NORTH AMERICAN WILDLIFE

MAMMALS, REPTILES, AND AMPHIBIANS

NORTH AMERICAN

WILDLIFE

MAMMALS, REPTILES, AND AMPHIBIANS

Reader's Digest

The Reader's Digest Association, Inc.
Pleasantville, New York/Montreal

A READER'S DIGEST BOOK

Edited and designed by Media Projects Incorporated

Editors:
Edward S. Barnard
Sharon Fass Yates

Managing Editor:
Lelia Mander

Assistant Editor:
Aaron Murray

Production Manager:
Laura Smyth

Design:
Design Oasis

Copy Editor:
Charlotte Maurer

Consultant for revised edition:
Robert E. Budliger
Dir. of Environmental
Education (retired)
NY State Department of
Environmental Conservation

The credits and acknowledgments that appear on page 191 are hereby made a part of this copyright page.

Library of Congress Cataloging in Publication Data
Mammals, reptiles, and amphibians.
   p. cm. (North American Wildlife)
  Includes Index.
  ISBN 0-7621-0035-4
   1. Mammals—North America—Identification. 2. Reptiles—North America—Identification. 3. Amphibians—North America—Identification. I. Reader's Digest Association.
QL715.N86 1998
599'.097—dc21   97-32724

This book contains revised material originally published in 1982 in the Reader's Digest book, NORTH AMERICAN WILDLIFE.

Printed in the United States of America
Second Printing, April 2000

CONTENTS

Mammals, Reptiles, and Amphibians is a book to browse through as well as a guide for identifying animals. Use it to learn about the elaborate courtship of the Brook Salamander, how the Mountain Lion hunts its prey, which North American lizard is the only venomous species in the world, and other fascinating facts. Use it also to distinguish the harmless Milk Snake from the dangerous Copperhead, or to recognize the ornate pattern of the Painted Turtle, the coral snake's vibrant rings, and the sleek lines of the Striped Chorus Frog. Unique in its coverage, this book identifies more than 230 of the most common, conspicuous, or important species of North American mammals, reptiles, and amphibians—from the tiny Southern Cricket Frog to the powerful Grizzly Bear.

Each of the book's three sections starts with an introduction that explains how the section is organized and provides general identification tips. The species entries are carefully written so that all the salient facts are easy to find. Information important for identification (size, markings, and the like) is in a compact **identification capsule**. The capsules are intended to be used together with the color portraits, for certain features mentioned in the capsules have been highlighted with check marks on the art. These **idento-checks** point out particular traits to look for when you're identifying a species.

In every section of this book there are certain species, such as Raccoons, that can be easily recognized. Where you find these animals doesn't much matter (for identification purposes, at least). For others, where you find them is often an important clue to identifying them. The **range maps** help out here. Much easier to use than lengthy written descriptions of ranges, these maps show the areas where particular species are likely to be found. Any animal will move about, so the ranges shown on the maps should be considered approximations only.

HELPFUL IDENTIFICATION FEATURES

Range maps show at a glance where the animal is likely to be found.

Titles provide **common names** and are always followed by **scientific names**.

Easy-to-locate **identification capsules** contain the facts most important for identification.

Text blocks are packed with interesting information and lore about the animal.

Many species have **boxed illustrations** showing such features as paw prints, webbed feet, scales, and underbelly markings.

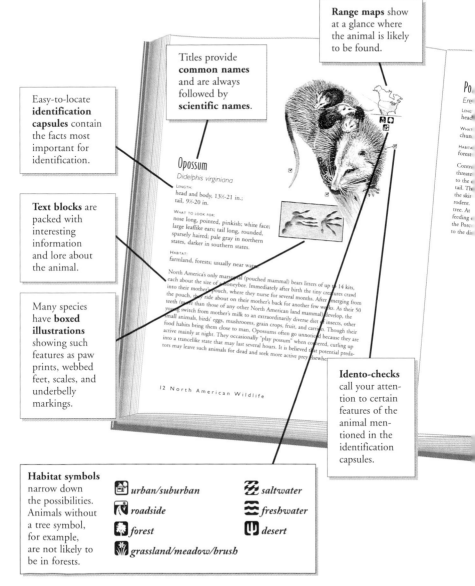

Opossum
Didelphis virginiana

LENGTH:
head and body, 13½-21 in.;
tail, 9½-20 in.

WHAT TO LOOK FOR:
nose long, pointed, pinkish; white face; large leaflike ears; tail long, rounded, sparsely haired; pale gray in northern states, darker in southern states.

HABITAT:
farmland, forests; usually near water.

North America's only marsupial (pouched mammal) bears litters of up to 14 kits, each about the size of a honeybee. Immediately after birth the tiny creatures crawl into their mother's pouch, where they nurse for several months. After emerging from the pouch, they ride about on their mother's back for another few weeks. As their 50 teeth (more than those of any other North American land mammal) develop, the young switch from mother's milk to an extraordinarily diverse diet of insects, other small animals, birds' eggs, mushrooms, grain crops, fruit, and carrion. Though their food habits bring them close to man, Opossums often go unnoticed because they are active mainly at night. They occasionally "play possum" when cornered, curling up into a trancelike state that may last several hours. It is believed that potential predators may leave such animals for dead and seek more active prey elsewhere.

12 North American Wildlife

Idento-checks call your attention to certain features of the animal mentioned in the identification capsules.

Po
Ere

LENG
head

WHAT
chun

HABITA
forest

Contr
threate
to the e
tail. Th
the skin
rodent.
tree. At
feeding e
the Porc
to the di

Habitat symbols narrow down the possibilities. Animals without a tree symbol, for example, are not likely to be in forests.

- *urban/suburban*
- *roadside*
- *forest*
- *grassland/meadow/brush*
- *saltwater*
- *freshwater*
- *desert*

MAMMALS

Although North America has some 400 species of mammals, most are by no means easy to find. True, Raccoons catch our attention when they prowl around our homes, and Bison are much too big to stay hidden in the grass. But the majority of mammals survive by being elusive. Many avoid the light of day (a behavior pattern that also keeps them cool). Opossums and Mink, for example, are primarily nocturnal; deer and rabbits are active mainly at dawn and dusk.

Another reason it is difficult to spot mammals is because they blend in with their environment. Their fur—a feature unique to mammals (another unique trait is that they nurse their young)—is usually some shade of brown and provides them with protective camouflage. In some species, such as the Varying Hare, the fur changes color with the seasons to achieve year-round camouflage. Stripes or other patterns often break the image into fragments or chunks so that a predator doesn't perceive the mammal as a whole (fawns are a prime example). Many mammals, and other animals too, are pale on the underside, which offsets any shadow that might make them stand out from their surroundings. And few mammals are noisy enough to attract your attention with sound.

With their high sensitivity to odor and sound, mammals often sense an approaching human in ample time for them to hide or flee. Whether predator or prey (often both), a mammal depends on a keen awareness of its surroundings, and anyone hoping to observe mammals in the wild must take this awareness into account. Specific dos and don'ts are provided on pages 10-11.

Searching for Mammals

To increase your chances of spotting mammals, don't just hope they'll pass your way; learn to be a detective. Look for clues to where they have been and where they might return to. Cracks or ridges running along the surface indicate mole tunnels below. Dome-shaped heaps of grasses in water say Muskrat.

Be alert too for food-related signs. Squirrels build up heaps of "used" pine cones. Mouse-like Pikas prepare winter larders—piles of dried plant materials. Bears and Porcupines leave tooth marks in trees. Tracks reveal the presence of mammal life. Although the form they take varies with the speed of the animal and with the surface (tracks in the snow look different from those in mud), certain species make very distinctive tracks. Some of these patterns are shown in this book alongside the animal that makes them. Look for animal footprints in the desert sand—and remember that mammals are creatures of habit who, once familiar with a certain place, tend to return to it again and again. In this way visible trails are created, whether by voles tunneling through the grass or deer traveling established routes.

Identifying Mammals

Mammals are, for the most part, more difficult to identify than birds; few have the distinctiveness of a Robin or a Cardinal, and there are a large number of little rodents that look pretty much alike. You should have little problem identifying mammals that you've had the luxury of observing out in the open for a long period of time. But if one crosses your path only briefly, try to extract from the encounter a general impression of its shape and color, and also a rough estimate of the size of its ears and the length of its tail. With such information at hand, you'll have a much easier time giving the creature a name.

Specific information about the habits of mammals shown in this book is given in the individual entries for each species. Closely related animals are generally grouped together; the hoofed mammals, for example, are shown on pages 66 through 69. There is, however, an exception: the species on the first two pages belong to several different groups.

TIPS ON OBSERVING MAMMALS

- Don't wear clothing that contrasts with the landscape; in a wooded area, for instance, wear browns and greens. Patterned fabrics like camouflage cloth break your image into smaller, less conspicuous parts. Choose clothing that doesn't rustle, and avoid fabrics, jewelry, and other items that reflect the sun.

- Keep your voice low, and move slowly. Take advantage of cover when approaching an animal or a viewing site (sometimes it's best to crawl on all fours). Stay away from open hilltops where you might be silhouetted against the sky. Don't make hand movements that will give you away.

- Don't smoke. To animals, the smell of tobacco means danger. Smokers and nonsmokers alike can give their clothes a natural aroma by storing them with pine needles for a day or two.

- If you plan to spend some time at a promising site, a folding stool or foam-rubber cushion will add to your comfort. Before you settle down, take note of the breeze and position yourself downwind.

- Encountering wild mammals can be a thrill in itself. But if you're lucky, you may be able to watch the animals doing something—feeding, drinking, interacting with you or with others of their own kind. The illustrations on these two pages show behavior you may observe.

Parental care. The females nurse their offspring, protect them, and keep them warm (sometimes the males help out too). Seals and sea lions breed in colonies that are out in the open, and they use the same sites year after year. Be sure to use binoculars and do your best not to disturb the colonies.

Play. It is the young animals who play. Often taking the form of wrestling or chasing, play is a repetitive, exuberant activity that helps the youngsters learn.

Threat behavior. Animals threaten in a way that focuses attention on their weaponry. Though few can observe the gesture with the proper scientific detachment, the Spotted Skunk's hand-stand is a threat, followed with a spray should the intruder not retreat. Moose lower their antlers; wolves bare their teeth. To observe threat gestures, you should listen as well. Opossums hiss; Porcupines gnash their teeth.

Fighting. Often preceded by threats, fighting occurs among males of many species as they establish territories or take possession of a female. The purpose of fighting is not to kill but to drive the opponent away. Small mammals wrestle and bite; Mountain Sheep use their horns.

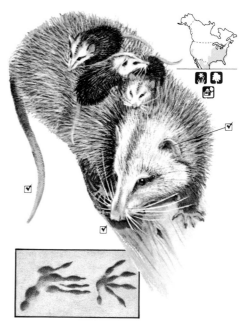

Opossum
Didelphis virginiana

LENGTH:
head and body, 13½-21 in.;
tail, 9½-20 in.

WHAT TO LOOK FOR:
nose long, pointed, pinkish; white face;
large leaflike ears; tail long, rounded,
sparsely haired; pale gray in northern
states, darker in southern states.

HABITAT:
farmland, forests; usually near water.

North America's only marsupial (pouched mammal) bears litters of up to 14 kits,
each about the size of a honeybee. Immediately after birth the tiny creatures crawl
into their mother's pouch, where they nurse for several months. After emerging from
the pouch, they ride about on their mother's back for another few weeks. As their 50
teeth (more than those of any other North American land mammal) develop, the
young switch from mother's milk to an extraordinarily diverse diet of insects, other
small animals, birds' eggs, mushrooms, grain crops, fruit, and carrion. Though their
food habits bring them close to man, Opossums often go unnoticed because they are
active mainly at night. They occasionally "play possum" when cornered, curling up
into a trancelike state that may last several hours. It is believed that potential predators may leave such animals for dead and seek more active prey elsewhere.

Porcupine

Erethizon dorsatum

LENGTH:
head and body, 18-23 in.; tail, 6-11 in.

WHAT TO LOOK FOR:
chunky body; short legs; long, stiff quills; slow-moving gait.

HABITAT:
forests (commonly in trees); occasionally in brushy areas.

Contrary to popular belief, the Porcupine does not shoot its quills. When threatened by the weasellike Fisher or some other predator, it turns its back to the enemy, raises its approximately 30,000 quills, and strikes out with its tail. The barbed quills, which are really modified hairs loosely attached to the skin, become embedded on contact. The Porcupine is a large nocturnal rodent. If seen during the day, it appears as a round, dark shape high in a tree. At night it clambers from tree to tree, often causing serious damage by feeding on buds, twigs, and bark. In areas where trappers have eliminated the Porcupine's predators, its population has increased dramatically—much to the dismay of foresters.

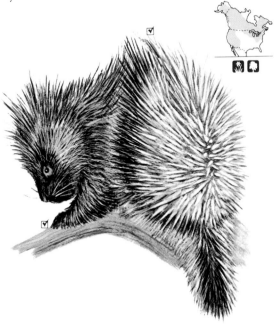

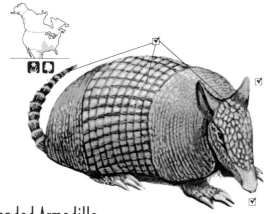

Nine-banded Armadillo

Dasypus novemcinctus

LENGTH:
head and body, 15-17½ in.; tail, 13 -15½ in.

WHAT TO LOOK FOR:
bony plates on body, tail, and top of head, large ears; long, squarish snout.

HABITAT:
brushy or rocky areas; forests (pines in East).

The armadillo's lizardlike skin and bony-plated shell look like the perfect defense against predators. Although on rare occasions the animal may curl into a ball when attacked, it is more likely to protect itself by quickly digging a hole or fleeing into its burrow. The burrow is a multichambered tunnel where the females give birth, always to quadruplets that are always of the same sex. Close relatives of anteaters and sloths, armadillos are extending their range.

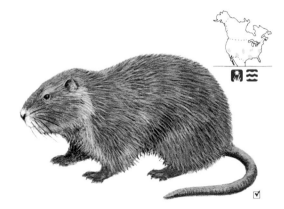

Nutria

Myocastor coypus

LENGTH:
head and body, 20-26 in.; tail, 12-17 in.

WHAT TO LOOK FOR:
grayish-brown rodent midway in size between a Muskrat and a Beaver; tail long, almost hairless, round (not flattened).

HABITAT:
freshwater marshes, ponds, lakes, swamps.

Native to South America, Nutrias, or Coypus, were brought to this continent in the 1930s. Some individuals escaped from fur ranches, others were released to control vegetation in lakes, and the species became part of the wildlife of North America. Though their diet, habitat, and fertility are similar to the Muskrat's, Nutrias are larger and highly competitive. In certain areas they have displaced the Muskrat, usurping its lodges, burrows, and feeding areas. Man and alligators are their main enemies.

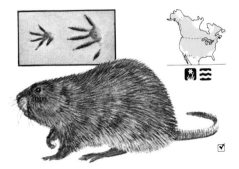

Muskrat

Ondatra zibethicus

LENGTH:
head and body, 9-15 in.; tail, 7½-10½ in.

WHAT TO LOOK FOR:
color reddish brown, except for light gray belly;
tail black, scaly, vertically flattened.

HABITAT:
marshes, ponds, lakes, slow streams with reeds
and cattails.

This aquatic mammal persists despite the widespread drainage of marshes,
for it can survive in a variety of wetland habitats. Its versatile diet is also
an asset; though it feeds mainly on aquatic plants, it also eats snails, clams,
crayfish, and frogs and may travel hundreds of feet from water to harvest
land plants. It reproduces rapidly—several litters a year, each with up to
11 young. Muskrats use aquatic lodges that are smaller than beaver lodges
and made of grasses and sedges instead of sticks and mud.

Beaver

Castor canadensis

LENGTH:
head and body, 27-38 in.; tail, 9-12 in.

WHAT TO LOOK FOR:
front teeth prominent, orange; tail large, paddlelike, scaly.

HABITAT:
lakes and streams bordered with poplars, birches,
or other food trees.

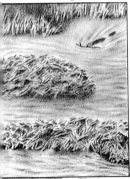

Beaver lodge and dam

Famed for their dam-building ability, North America's largest
rodents begin by making an underwater foundation of mud and
stone. Then they gnaw down trees, leaving characteristic cone-
shaped stumps, and drag or float cuttings to the dam site, where
they are incorporated into the foundation with more mud. As a
pond forms behind the dam, the pair of Beavers build a stick-and-
mud lodge with underwater entrances and an inside platform raised
above the water. Here they remain much of the day, emerging at
dusk to forage for succulent plants or to cut trees and shrubs. In
late summer and fall the cuttings are stored in an underwater food
pile, to be eaten in winter. The kits are born in spring and stay in
the home pond until they are two years old.

Little Brown Bat

Myotis lucifugus

SIZE:
length, 3-4½ in.; wingspan, 8-10 in.

WHAT TO LOOK FOR:
low, zigzagging flight; small size;
dark, shiny fir.

HABITAT:
flies near wooded areas and water; roosts
in caves, hollow trees, buildings.

Probably the most abundant bat in North America, this mammal is common in
and around cities. On summer days thousands may hang upside down in an attic
or loft. These sleeping groups are composed solely of females and young, for Little
Brown Bats, like many other species, separate by sex before the young are born.
Males also roost during the day but usually as solitary individuals.

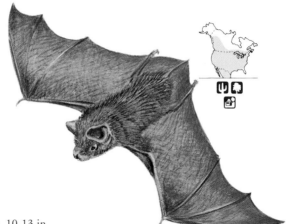

Big Brown Bat

Eptesicus fuscus

SIZE:
length, 3½-5 in.; wingspan, 10-13 in.

WHAT TO LOOK FOR:
strong, steady flight; large size.

HABITAT:
flies in forests; roosts in caves, hollow trees, buildings
(especially in summer).

Occasionally seen flying during the day, Big Brown Bats usually emerge at twilight
to pursue prey over meadows, suburban streets, and city traffic. They detect beetles
and other insects by emitting high-pitched sounds that bounce off objects and
come back as echoes. The same technique, known as echolocation and used by
other insect-eating bats, also helps them avoid obstacles.

Identifying bats.

Flying bats are difficult to identify. Although size and shape
supply some clues, often only an educated guess is possible—
and only after finding out which species are likely to be
around. Roosting bats present fewer problems. In checking
them, however, remember that bats should never be handled
with bare hands. All are believed to be able to transmit rabies.

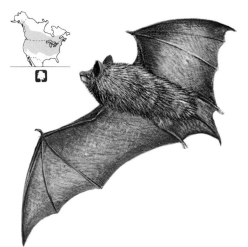

Silver-haired Bat

Lasionycteris noctivagans

SIZE:
length, 4-4½ in.; wingspan, 10-12½ in.

WHAT TO LOOK FOR:
flight relatively high, straight, and slow; fur dark,
with white tips on back.

HABITAT:
flies in forests; roosts mainly in trees near water.

Although most North American bats give birth to a single
young, this species produces twins. (The tree-roosting Red
Bat, *Lasiurus borealis*, occasionally has quadruplets.) Bats
give birth while hanging at their roosts, then nurse their offspring for several weeks. Young ones cling to their mothers'
bellies until they can fly independently.

Brazilian Free-tailed Bat

Tadarida brasiliensis

SIZE:
length, 3½-4 in.; wingspan, 11-13 in.

WHAT TO LOOK FOR:
flight high, straight, fast; long tail.

HABITAT:
roosts in buildings and caves, especially in
Carlsbad Caverns, New Mexico.

Bats are the only true flying mammals. They wing through the
air on thin membranes stretched between their elongated
"fingers." A smaller membrane usually connects the hind limbs
and spans the tail, which extends well beyond the membrane in
free-tailed bats. This bat summers in enormous numbers in
southwestern caves and winters in Mexico. Most bats in
temperate regions hibernate in winter.

Star-nosed Mole

Condylura cristata

LENGTH:
head and body, 4½-5 in.; tail, 2½-3½ in.

WHAT TO LOOK FOR:
nose large, pinkish, with fleshy projections; long hairy tail.

HABITAT:
moist, low-lying soil.

This burrowing mammal is equally at home in water and on land. Frequently its winding tunnels end in a pond or stream. An excellent swimmer, the Star-nosed Mole uses its broad front feet as paddles and its thick tail as a scull. It dives after much of its food—aquatic insects, crustaceans, snails, and even small fish. Excess food is converted into fat and stored in its tail, to be used as an energy source during times of scarcity. The 22 projections on its nose are sensitive feelers, which help it locate prey; the two round holes in the center are the nostrils. Moles characteristically have a highly developed sense of touch, but their eyesight is poor.

Broad-footed Mole
Scapanus latimanus

LENGTH:
head and body, 5½-6½ in.; tail, 1½-2 in.

WHAT TO LOOK FOR:
front feet greater in width than in length; fur blackish brown
to black; tail nearly hairless.

HABITAT:
soft soil in meadows and forests.

Active night and day beneath the surface, the Broad-footed, or
California, Mole seems to swim through the soil as it tunnels along,
wedging its spindle-shaped body into the sod. Its powerful feet act as
shovels; its fleshy nose packs the dirt. Earthworms and other prey are
detected by their vibrations. Like other moles, the Broad-footed species
has an extremely high metabolic rate, causing the animal to burn up so
much food that it must eat its own weight in food every day. This mole
resembles two other western species—the Townsend's Mole (*Scapanus
townsendii*) and the Coast Mole (*Scapanus orarius*).

Eastern Mole

Scalopus aquaticus

LENGTH:
head and body, 4½-6½ in.; tail, 1-1½ in.

WHAT TO LOOK FOR:
soft, velvety fur, gray in north, golden
to darker brown elsewhere; hairless tail.

HABITAT:
moist, sandy soils in grassy areas.

The Eastern Mole spends most of its life beneath the surface of the earth. After a rain it moves through shallow tunnels, searching for earthworms, insect larvae, and other prey. Its permanent passageway, which lies 10 inches or more beneath the surface, is also a retreat during drought or cold spells. Moles are not hibernators, and remain active throughout the winter. Notorious for their inability to tolerate others of their kind (chance encounters sometimes lead to death), they are solitary except during the breeding season. Eastern Moles mate in spring. Four weeks later the female, which is slightly smaller than the male, gives birth in an underground nest lined with dried plant material. Raised ridges in the soil (pushed up as the mole tunnels along) and molehills (mounds of excavated earth) are more likely to be seen than the animal itself. Though moles may wreak havoc on a lawn, they do accomplish some good by eating insects and aerating the soil.

Masked Shrew

Sorex cinereus

LENGTH:
head and body, 1¾-2½ in.; tail, 1-2 in.

WHAT TO LOOK FOR:
grayish-brown color; tail longer than that of other shrews.

HABITAT:
moist soil in grasslands, brushy areas, and forests.

This tiny bundle of fierce energy, also called the Common Shrew, is found in a greater variety of habitats than any other North American mammal. Throughout the northern part of the continent it seems equally at home in grassy fields, salt marshes, coniferous forests, and high mountain slopes. Active at any hour (though more so at night than during the day), it furiously searches for food and eats more than its weight each day in insects, mollusks, earthworms, and occasionally carrion. It is not much of a burrower and often hunts in tunnels dug by other mammals. Like other shrews, this species does not hibernate but is active throughout the year. Several litters of up to 10 young are produced each year from spring until fall. Few live for much more than a year.

Moles versus shrews.

People occasionally confuse these two groups of mammals.
Here's how to tell them apart:

- **Overall shape.** Moles are larger and fatter. Shrews are mouse-size or smaller.
- **Snout.** Both groups have long snouts. The mole's is naked and pink; the shrew's is furred nearly to the tip.
- **Eyes.** Eyes are small in both groups but minuscule in moles. Certain moles are blind, with skin covering their eyes.
- **Feet.** Unlike shrews, moles have huge front feet; the soles face outward.
- **Tails.** Mole tails are stubby and can be either haired or hairless (this varies according to species). Most shrews have longer, thinner tails with stiff hairs.

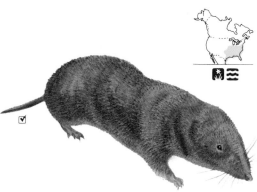

Least Shrew
Cryptotis parva

LENGTH:
head and body, 2-2½ in.; tail, ½-¾ in.

WHAT TO LOOK FOR:
cinnamon brown color; very short tail.

HABITAT:
open fields, freshwater marshes, sparse brush.

Also known as the Bee Shrew, this very small mammal occasionally nests in beehives and feeds on bees and their larvae. More frequently it nests in fallen leaves and utilizes the surface runways of voles as it searches, nose aquiver, for insects and other small prey. Its digestion, like that of other shrews, is remarkably rapid; the hard parts of insects pass through its alimentary tract in about 90 minutes. Shrews are the world's smallest mammals and form an important intermediate link in the food chain, serving as food for such animals as owls, hawks, and snakes. There are about 30 kinds of shrews in North America, but many of them are restricted to rather small areas.

Sorting out small mammals.

At first glance, many small mammals look similar because of their size. However, closer observation reveals important differences among the shrews, voles, lemmings, mice, and rats:

- **Shape.** Shrews have elongated bodies and pointed noses. Voles and lemmings are stocky and rounded, with little separation between head and body. The heads of mice and rats are better defined.
- **Ears.** The ears of mice and rats are prominent. Those of voles and lemmings are somewhat obscured by long, soft fur; those of shrews are almost imperceptible.
- **Eyes.** Mice and rats have large eyes; voles and lemmings, small beady ones; and shrews even smaller ones.
- **Tails.** In proportion to the rest of the animal, the tails of mice and rats are long;those of shrews, voles, and lemmings are usually shorter.

Short-tailed Shrew

Blarina brevicauda

LENGTH:
head and body, 3-4 in.; tail, ¾-1 in.

WHAT TO LOOK FOR:
dark metallic gray color; relatively short tail.

HABITAT:
all land habitats except deserts.

This abundant species is unique among North American mammals in having venomous saliva, which probably aids it in subduing mice and other mammals that equal or surpass it in size. More shrewlike is its habit of eating insects, including many pests; Short-tailed Shrews are believed to have killed 60 percent of the Larch Sawfly larvae in eastern Canada. This shrew has two breeding seasons, one in spring and one in fall. During these periods males pursue females, making clicking sounds during the chase; an unreceptive female rebuffs her suitor with loud squeaks and chattering. Litters of up to eight furless young are born three weeks after mating, and weaning occurs after another three weeks.

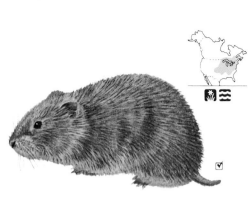

Southern Bog Lemming
Synaptomys cooperi

LENGTH:
head and body, 3½-4½ in.;
tail, ½-¾ in.

WHAT TO LOOK FOR:
back brownish gray, belly gray;
tail short; ears nearly hidden.

HABITAT:
bogs and wet meadows with thick
vegetation.

Volelike in habits and appearance, the Southern Bog Lemming is a social rodent that lives in colonies of from several to several dozen animals. It is also found in the company of other small mammals, including voles, shrews, and moles, and may utilize their runways and burrows. It feeds mainly on leaves and stems but also relishes berries, seeds, bark, and insects. Similar in appearance but slightly larger is the Northern Bog Lemming (*Synaptomys borealis*), an inhabitant of wet mountain areas across much of Canada. The Brown Lemming (*Lemmus sibiricus*) lives on the tundra farther north. Lemmings in Scandinavia are famous for their periodic population explosions, which often result in mass migrations.

Woodland Vole
Microtus pinetorum

LENGTH:
head and body, 3-4 in.; tail, ½-1 in.

WHAT TO LOOK FOR:
soft fur, reddish brown on back,
gray below; very short tail.

HABITAT:
forest floors covered with thick duff
(decaying vegetation); orchards.

Meadow Vole

Microtus pennsylvanicus

LENGTH:
head and body, 3½-5 in.; tail, 1½-2½ in.

WHAT TO LOOK FOR:
back and sides brown to dark brown;
gray below.

HABITAT:
grasslands with dense vegetation;
open forests, orchards, forest edges.

Runways of closely cropped grasses reveal the comings and goings of the Meadow Vole, or Field Mouse, a stocky creature with some impressive statistics. Populations frequently number several hundred per acre and during one "mouse plague" reached an estimated 10,000 per acre. A female can produce a hundred young within just one year. These prolific rodents may be highly destructive to hay and other forage crops, but they are an important food supply for birds of prey and small carnivorous mammals.

◀ Woodland Vole (AT LEFT) The smallest North American vole, also called the Pine Vole, lives among pines only in the South; elsewhere it prefers broad-leaved forests, especially where the soil is loose. Though the Woodland Vole tunnels through leaf litter at the surface, it also burrows to depths of 12 inches. It has a rather short tail, short ears, soft fur, small eyes, and strong front feet—all adaptations to a subterranean way of life. The underground parts of plants are its usual diet; these include not only wild plants but—to the dismay of farmers—peanuts and potatoes as well.

Southern Red-backed Vole

Clethrionomys gapperi

LENGTH:
head and body, 3½-4½ in.; tail, 1-2 in.

WHAT TO LOOK FOR:
back reddish brown, sides grayer, belly whitish; sometimes gray all over.

HABITAT:
forests, usually in moist areas.

With a trotting gait this small creature, also known as the Red-backed Vole, moves rapidly along the forest floor. An agile climber, it scrambles over fallen tree trunks and even up living ones to feed or seek out nest sites; it has been known to kill trees of up to a foot in diameter by gnawing the bark. Though it has many predators (as do other small rodents), it reproduces so prolifically that it is often the most abundant mammal on the forest floor.

Hispid Pocket Mouse

Chaetodipus hispidus

LENGTH:
head and body, 4½-5 in.; tail, 3½-4½ in.

WHAT TO LOOK FOR:
relatively large size; tannish brown above, whitish below; coarse hair.

HABITAT:
grassy areas; along roads and fences.

Meadow Jumping Mouse

Zapus hudsonius

MEADOW JUMPING MOUSE

WESTERN JUMPING MOUSE

LENGTH:
head and body, 3-3½ in.; tail, 4½-6 in.

WHAT TO LOOK FOR:
yellowish brown above, white below; large hind feet; tail long, sparsely haired.

HABITAT:
meadows, clearings.

Using its long tail for balance and its long hind legs to spring into the air, the Meadow Jumping Mouse can leap across distances of 5 feet or more. Primarily nocturnal, this diminutive creature evades owls, weasels, and other predators with a zigzagging series of jumps across meadow and field. Unlike most mice, it uses a burrow not for year-round refuge but only during its winter-long hibernation. A grassy nest in a tussock or beneath a log serves as its nursery and summer shelter. Meadow Jumping Mice mate soon after waking in spring; litters averaging about five blind, hairless young are born several weeks later. They breed again in late summer. A closely related species, the Western Jumping Mouse (*Zapus princeps*), bears but one litter a year.

◄ **Hispid Pocket Mouse** (AT LEFT) Pocket mice carry seeds to their burrows in expandable pouches on the outside of their cheeks. Once inside the burrows—usually dug with the entrance beneath a shrub—they force out the seeds by pressing against the pouches with their front feet. Pocket mice seldom, if ever, drink water, evidently depending on the "metabolic water" produced as they digest their food. All 20 or so species of pocket mice are found in dry regions west of the Mississippi. Similar in general appearance and habits (all are active only at night), they vary in size, color, and the texture of their fur. The Hispid Pocket Mouse (*hispid* means "bristly") is the largest of the pocket mice.

Northern Grasshopper Mouse

Onychomys leucogaster

LENGTH: head and body, 4½-5½ in.; tail, 1-2½ in.

WHAT TO LOOK FOR: plump body; short tail; gray or cinnamon above, white below; white feet and tip of tail.

HABITAT: prairies, deserts.

GRAY PHASE

CINNAMON PHASE

A veritable tiger among mice, this nocturnal rodent feeds not only on grasshoppers but also on beetles, crickets, caterpillars, spiders, lizards, and small mammals. The larger prey is stalked, seized with a rush, and then killed with a bite on the neck. Because of its taste for scorpions, it is sometimes called the Scorpion Mouse, as is the Southern Grasshopper Mouse (*Onychomys torridus*), a smaller creature with a more southerly range. Grasshopper mice nest in burrows, often preempting those made by other small rodents. Occasionally they are spotted standing on their hind feet and pointing their noses into the air, uttering shrill sounds at the same time.

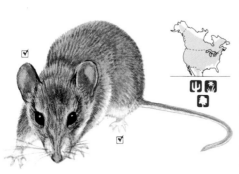

Deer Mouse

Peromyscus maniculatus

LENGTH: head and body, 3-4 in.; tail, 2-5 in.

WHAT TO LOOK FOR: white feet and belly; tail dark above, white below; prominent ears.

HABITAT: nearly every habitat except very wet places; will enter buildings.

Deer Mice and deer have little in common except the dark-above, light-below pattern of their fur. Varying in color from region to region, the Deer Mouse is one of the most widely distributed mammals in North America. It is a social creature, with groups of up to a dozen or more huddling together in winter. Active throughout the year, Deer Mice depend on stored seeds for survival in winter. They are nocturnal and usually rest during the day in burrows, trees, buildings, and even bird nests.

Plains Harvest Mouse

Reithrodontomys montanus

LENGTH:
head and body, 2½-3 in.; tail, 2-2½ in.

WHAT TO LOOK FOR:
small size; pale grayish to tan above,
lighter below; faint stripe on back.

HABITAT:
uplands with low-growing plants.

This little mouse is a versatile reaper, bending stalks of grass downward to nibble at the fruiting tips or picking up seeds from the ground. It is also a weaver, shaping grass into a round nest. Located on the ground or slightly above it in a bush or thick grass, the nest may be abandoned in cold weather for a burrow. North America has five kinds of harvest mice, which together range over most of the lower 48 states. All look much like the common House Mouse. A good way of telling harvest mice from the House Mouse—but one that involves capturing the creature in question—is to look at the teeth. Only the harvest mice have a vertical groove on each upper incisor.

House Mouse

Mus musculus

LENGTH:
head and body, 3-3½ in.; tail, 2½-4 in.

WHAT TO LOOK FOR:
dull color (grayish brown on back, gray
below); long, scaly tail; prominent ears.

HABITAT:
around buildings.

This uninvited house guest thrives not only on food intended for man but also on such prosaic items as soap and glue. For nest material it helps itself to anything soft, including pillow feathers and shredded newspapers. Like many pest species, the House Mouse is not native to North America. Originally from Asia, it first reached the New World as a 16th-century stowaway from Europe. Its reproductive capacity is enormous. Under certain conditions a female may produce eight litters a year, with up to a dozen young in a single litter. The mice are ready to breed when little more than a month old.

Ord's Kangaroo Rat
Dipodomys ordii

LENGTH:
head and body, 4-4½ in.; tail, 5-6 in.

WHAT TO LOOK FOR:
large size; long hind legs; long, striped, tufted tail; small ears; light patch behind eye.

HABITAT:
dry, sandy areas.

Often seen hopping across a road at night, this long-legged leaper can make a sharp turn in midair and cover 2 feet in a single bound. This species is the most widespread of the kangaroo rats—rodents noteworthy not only for their jumping ability but also for their seed-carrying technique. Like pocket mice, they stuff seeds into external cheek pouches (the openings are on the outside of the cheeks) and carry the food into burrows, storing it there for later use. Burrows also serve as nurseries and provide daytime relief from the desert sun. Kangaroo rats obtain most of the water they need as a product of digestion.

Florida Woodrat
Neotoma floridana

LENGTH:
head and body, 8-9 in.; tail, 6-8 in.

WHAT TO LOOK FOR:
soft fur; grayish brown above, white below (including tail); tail furred, shorter than rest of animal.

HABITAT:
usually in open places, including swamps and rocky areas.

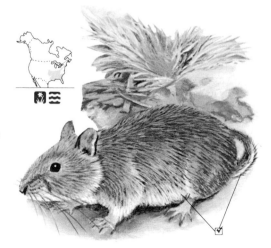

Bushy-tailed Woodrat

Neotoma cinerea

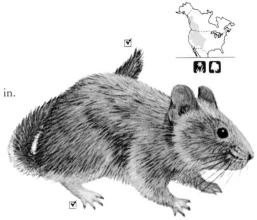

LENGTH:
head and body, 7-10 in.; tail, 5-7½ in.

WHAT TO LOOK FOR:
tail bushy (though less so than a squirrel's); pale reddish gray to black above, white below (including tail); white feet.

HABITAT:
rocky areas, coniferous forests.

Occasionally a camper falls victim to a peculiar "theft"—some small trinket is stolen and a stick or stone left in its place. The culprit is likely to be a woodrat, a soft-furred rodent also known as a trade rat or packrat. Woodrats do not really trade objects but may drop items they are carrying in order to pick up something else. Stolen items are incorporated into stick-and-bone nests, often constructed in rock crevices or shrubbery. The Bushy-tailed Woodrat has a relatively modest nest compared with that of the Dusky-footed Woodrat (*Neotoma fuscipes*). Built in trees or on the ground, the impressive stick tower of this California resident may measure some 6 feet tall.

◀ **Florida Woodrat** (AT LEFT) When threatened or otherwise excited, the Florida Woodrat chatters its teeth, vibrates its tail against the ground, and thumps its hind feet. (Certain rabbits and mice also drum on the ground.) This rodent is usually solitary, living alone in a bulky nest built in a rock crevice or under a shrub. Young woodrats, two to four per litter, are nursed in the nest until about four weeks old; the mother's elongated teat fits into a gap between the two top front teeth of the newborn, an adaptation that helps her to carry them about. Adult woodrats feed on fruit, seeds, and nuts, and do man no economic harm, although some people dislike them merely because of their name and appearance.

Hispid Cotton Rat

Sigmodon hispidus

LENGTH:
head and body, 6-8 in.; tail, 3½-5½ in.

WHAT TO LOOK FOR:
fur long, coarse; dark brown mixed with buff, whitish below; inconspicuous ears.

HABITAT:
moist meadows, ditches.

This abundant rodent is named for the coarse, or hispid, quality of its fur. Common in farmlands, it damages cotton, alfalfa, and other crops and is regarded as a serious agricultural pest. Like many other rats, it adjusts its diet according to availability; for example, cotton rats in ditches sometimes feed almost exclusively on crayfish and fiddler crabs. Because cotton rats tend to have small home ranges, numerous individuals may occur in close proximity. One count revealed 513 cotton rats in a single rat-ridden acre, although the usual number is only about a dozen.

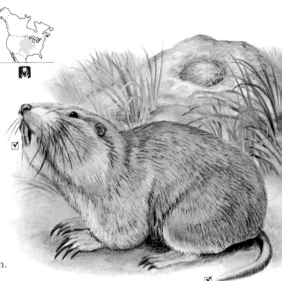

Plains Pocket Gopher
Geomys bursarius

LENGTH:
head and body, 5½-9 in.; tail, 2-4½ in.

WHAT TO LOOK FOR:
chunky body; tail short, nearly hairless;
prominent yellow teeth.

HABITAT:
grasslands, pastures, prairies.

Pocket gophers' pockets are outside cheek pouches, invisible unless crammed
with roots, bulbs, or other food. These burrowing rodents live solitary lives
(except during the brief spring mating season) and will battle any other
gopher that invades their home. Fan-shaped mounds marking tunnel
openings are common sights in gopher territory. Pocket gophers are easily
distinguished from most other mammals, for their teeth are visible even
when their mouths are closed. About 18 species in 3 genera, 8 of them in
Geomys, are recognized scientifically, although telling one from another is
a task for a specialist. The Plains Pocket Gopher, for example, is the only
species with two distinct grooves on the outside of each upper incisor.

Norway Rat
Rattus norvegicus

LENGTH:
head and body, 7-10 in.; tail, 5½-8 in.

WHAT TO LOOK FOR:
coarse fur; dull gray-brown above, paler (but not white) below;
tail long, scaly, nearly hairless, not bicolored.

HABITAT:
buildings, wharves, dumps; sometimes in fields.

Originally from Asia, the world's most destructive mammal reached North America
by ship about 1775. It has been an economic and a health problem since that time.
The Norway Rat eats almost anything of proper size, plant or animal, dead or alive.
It spreads disease and contaminates food. It has a high reproductive rate—an average
of 5 litters a year, with 8 to 10 rats in a litter. The Black, or Roof, Rat (*Rattus rattus*),
also native to Asia, usually stays close to seaports. Though its fur is darker and its tail
somewhat longer, the distinction is unimportant in human terms; the Black Rat
would probably cause as much destruction if the Norway Rat did not drive it away.

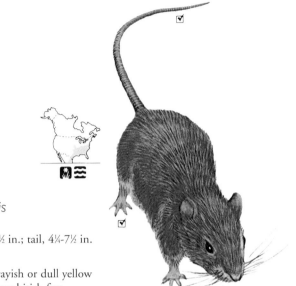

Marsh Rice Rat
Oryzomys palustris

LENGTH:
head and body, 4½-5½ in.; tail, 4¼-7½ in.

WHAT TO LOOK FOR:
gray-brown above, grayish or dull yellow
below; tail long, scaly; whitish feet.

HABITAT:
marshes; other wet or moist areas with
grasses or sedges.

As its name implies, the rice rat thrives on the tender shoots and ripened
grain of rice and other plants. It also eats fish and snails. Though generally
nocturnal, this slender rodent may feed at any hour and is active throughout
the year. Rice rats are semiaquatic, often diving and swimming a considerable
distance underwater when alarmed. They are vulnerable to predatory attacks
in the water (from Water Moccasins and Mink), on the land (skunks and
weasels), and from the sky (hawks and owls). The young are born in a nest
of dry leaves, which is usually perched a foot or more above the high-water
level in a tangle of rushes or other plants. Breeding may occur at any time of
year in the southern part of its range.

Red Squirrel
Tamiasciurus hudsonicus

LENGTH:
head and body, 7½-8½ in.; tail, 4-6 in.

WHAT TO LOOK FOR:
rusty above, whitish below; smaller than Gray Squirrel; tail less bushy.

HABITAT:
northern and mountain forests.

These noisy rodents, which announce an intruder with a harsh, strident call, are especially active just after sunrise and just before sunset. In midsummer they spend much of their time cutting cones from pines, spruces, and other trees and carrying them to caches near a log, under a tree, or in a burrow. The seeds in the cones will serve as food during the next winter. Red Squirrels are able to eat certain mushrooms that are deadly to man. Their diversified diet also includes buds, sap, and even bird eggs and nestlings. The squirrels are in turn an important food source for birds of prey.

Squirrel language.

Gray Squirrels are noisy. Although some vocalizations are probably idle chatter, others have a specific meaning:
- A rapid *kuk, kuk, kuk* means immediate danger.
- A drawn-out *ku-u-uk,* sounded at 2-second intervals, warns of less immediate danger.
- A slow *kuk-kuk-kuk* indicates the danger has passed.

Gray Squirrels convey a variety of messages with their tails:
- Rapid jerks are a threat gesture.
- Rapid waves (looser than jerks) are a sign of agitation.
- Holding the tail against the back may mean that danger has passed.

NORTHERN
FLYING
SQUIRREL

SOUTHERN
FLYING
SQUIRREL

Southern Flying Squirrel

Glaucomys volans

LENGTH:
head and body, 5½-6 in.; tail, 3½-5 in.

WHAT TO LOOK FOR:
grayish brown on back, white below; folds of skin between
front and back legs; large eyes.

HABITAT:
broad-leaved and mixed forests.

A flying squirrel cannot truly fly. It glides downward, using wide flaps of skin
along its sides to help slow its descent. To become airborne, this mammal
leaps and spreads its legs; to control the glide, it moves its legs and uses its
tail as a rudder. Immediately after a flying squirrel lands (usually 20 to 30
feet from its starting point), it may scramble to the far side of the tree—just
in case an owl is in pursuit. Like owls, flying squirrels are nocturnal. All other
North American squirrels are active during the day.

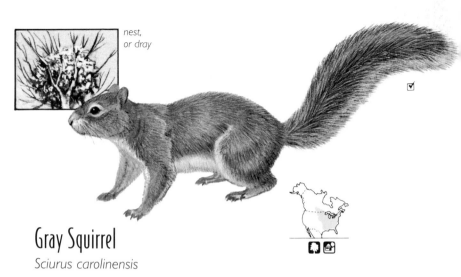

nest,
or dray

Gray Squirrel
Sciurus carolinensis

LENGTH:
head and body, 8-11 in.; tail, 8-10 in.

WHAT TO LOOK FOR:
usually gray on back and sides, whitish below (many northern ones are all black); large, bushy tail.

HABITAT:
broad-leaved forests, parks, suburbs.

Gray Squirrels breed twice a year, an event accompanied by fights, chases, and other noisy activities. Late winter or spring litters are usually born in tree hollows; summer ones, sometimes in leafy nests out along the branches of a tree. Males play no role in raising the young, which average three per litter and nurse for several months. Both the Gray Squirrel and its western relative (*Sciurus griseus*) are active all year, relying on buried food (as well as stolen birdseed) for winter sustenance.

Black-tailed Prairie Dog

Cynomys ludovicianus

LENGTH:
head and body, 10-14 in.; tail, 3-4 in.

WHAT TO LOOK FOR:
broad head; fat, yellowish-brown body; black-tipped tail.

HABITAT:
short- and mixed-grass prairies.

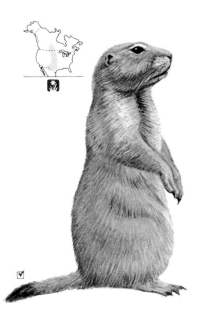

Not a dog at all, this stocky rodent takes its name from its bark, an alarm signal that sends all in the vicinity scurrying into their burrows. A prairie dog burrow is an elaborate network of tunnels at the base of a plunge shaft, which sometimes extends more than a dozen feet below the surface. Black-tailed Prairie Dogs are noted for their colonies ("towns"), which formerly covered many square miles and contained millions of inhabitants. Towns are divided into territories, each used by a group commonly dominated by a single male. The members of a group share their burrows, groom one another, and communicate through a variety of gestures and sounds. White-tailed Prairie Dogs (*Cynomys leucurus*) are less social.

Eastern Chipmunk
Tamias striatus

LENGTH:
head and body, 5½-6½ in.; tail, 3-4½ in.

WHAT TO LOOK FOR:
stripes on head, sides, and back; back
stripes extend only to rump.

HABITAT:
forests, brushy areas, gardens.

Chipmunks are ground-dwelling squirrels. They spend most of their lives at or below the
surface, although they will also climb trees. Their extensive burrows are up to 12 feet long
and may include a storage chamber, sleeping room, dump, and latrine, along with several
concealed entrances. The pantry holds up to half a bushel of nuts and other food, all
carried there in the chipmunk's outsized cheek pouches. Eastern Chipmunks partially
hibernate in winter (they wake frequently and feed). The females give birth in spring or
midsummer, producing litters of two to eight young. Like other members of the squirrel
family, chipmunks are naked, blind, and helpless at birth.

Thirteen-lined Ground Squirrel
Spermophilus tridecemlineatus

LENGTH:
head and body, 4½-6½ in.; tail, 2-5 in.

WHAT TO LOOK FOR:
many stripes on sides and back (some broken
into dots); small ears.

HABITAT:
brushy areas, overgrown fields, small stands
of trees, open areas.

Least Chipmunk
Tamias minimus

LENGTH:
head and body, 3½-4½ in.; tail, 3-4½ in.

WHAT TO LOOK FOR:
small, slim body; stripes on head, sides, and back; back stripes extend to base of tail.

HABITAT:
varied; includes tundra, forests, forest edges, sagebrush.

The smallest chipmunks are among the most active, scurrying over the ground and occasionally into trees. Piles of fruit pulp and nut trimmings mark their feeding sites. Least Chipmunks hibernate underground in winter and mate in spring. About a month later the female gives birth to a litter with up to seven young, which remain with her for several months. The Least Chipmunk is one of more than a dozen species of western chipmunks. Usually smaller and grayer than the Eastern Chipmunk, they vary in color according to their location. Desert inhabitants tend to be paler than forest ones, and individuals living in sun-dappled forests tend to have well-defined stripes.

◄ **Thirteen-lined Ground Squirrel** (AT LEFT) This is the Federation Squirrel, so called because of its pattern of "stars and stripes." Ground squirrels are burrowing animals, using their underground labyrinths as nurseries, hibernation dens, and temporary refuges. Active during the day, they retreat to their burrows at night and when skies are overcast. The Golden-mantled Ground Squirrel (*Spermophilus lateralis*), often seen around campgrounds in western parks, is sometimes confused with a chipmunk. Larger than any chipmunk, it has a single stripe on each side of the body but none on the head.

Woodchuck (Groundhog)
Marmota monax

LENGTH:
head and body, 14-20 in.;
tail, 4½-6½ in.

WHAT TO LOOK FOR:
large head; chunky body; short legs;
small bushy tail; no special markings.

HABITAT:
open forests, forest edges, rocky areas,
roadsides.

Contrary to legend, the Woodchuck, or
Groundhog, does not emerge from its burrow on February 2 to look for its shadow
or anything else. Instead, this stocky
rodent usually hibernates in its burrow (an
extensive system of tunnels, chambers, and
multiple entrances) until late winter. Soon
after emerging, male Woodchucks battle one another, using their teeth as weapons, and
then seek out the females. The young are born four weeks after mating. Although blind,
hairless, and extremely small at birth, they are ready for sorties outside the burrow within
a month. Adults are frequently seen sunbathing atop the entrance mound, sitting upright
on guard for predators, or waddling along as they stuff themselves with clover, alfalfa,
and other plants.

Pika
Ochotona princeps

LENGTH:
head and body, 6½-8½ in.

WHAT TO LOOK FOR:
ratlike head and body; small,
rounded ears; no visible tail.

HABITAT:
rock-strewn slopes.

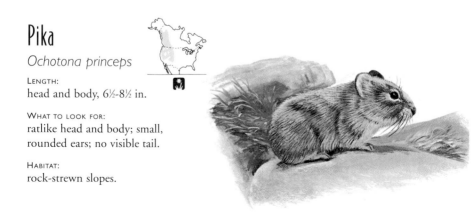

Yellow-bellied Marmot
Marmota flaviventris

LENGTH:
head and body, 14-20 in.; tail, 5½-8½ in.

WHAT TO LOOK FOR:
bulky body; white markings on dark face; bushy tail.

HABITAT:
rocky slopes, valleys.

Unlike the Woodchuck, the Yellow-bellied Marmot is a social animal, living in colonies of several dozen individuals. Often one marmot seems to be doing sentry duty while others in the colony graze in the alpine meadows. At the approach of danger (an eagle, for example), the sentry whistles sharply, causing marmots within earshot to scamper toward their burrows. Burrow entrances are usually located beneath rocks, so this large rodent is also known as the Rockchuck. A second species—the larger, grayer Hoary Marmot (*Marmota caligata*)— lives at higher elevations and is found farther north. Both species hibernate for more than half the year. Rockchucks may also become torpid and remain underground in hot weather.

◀ Pika (AT LEFT) The Pika, or Coney, harvests a variety of plants during the short mountain summer, stacks them in piles to cure in the sun, and eventually moves the "hay" to sheltered sites among the rocks. Between forays the little mammal dozes in the sunshine, nearly invisible as it sits hunched on a rock. Although the Pika looks like a rodent, it is technically a cousin of rabbits and hares. It remains active all winter, as do its relatives, but only the Pika stores hay for winter use. Much more vocal than rabbits and hares, the Pika communicates with others of its kind by sharp, nasal bleats and is occasionally called the Whistling, or Piping, Hare. It is some-thing of a ventriloquist—a skill to keep in mind when trying to locate the animal by its calls.

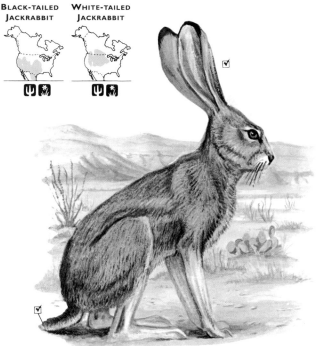

BLACK-TAILED JACKRABBIT   WHITE-TAILED JACKRABBIT

Black-tailed Jackrabbit

Lepus californicus

LENGTH:
head and body, 17-21 in.; tail, 4 in.

WHAT TO LOOK FOR:
ears very long, black-tipped; large hindfeet; dark streak on tail.

HABITAT:
grasslands, deserts.

The Black-tailed Jackrabbit is superbly adapted to life in open places. Relying on its speed to flee Coyotes and other predators, it can leap across distances of up to 20 feet and cover the ground at 30 to 35 miles an hour. During the day it rests in slight depressions, called forms, beneath shrubs, beside rocks, or in long grass. Its long ears act as antennas and air conditioners, picking up sound and dissipating body heat. The White-tailed Jackrabbit (*Lepus townsendii*) is similar in appearance but turns white in winter. The Antelope Jackrabbit (*Lepus alleni*), found mainly in Mexico, has even larger ears. All jackrabbits are technically hares, not rabbits.

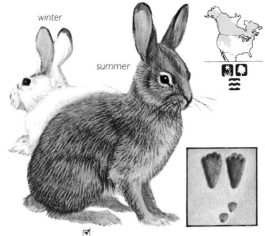

winter

summer

Snowshoe Hare ☑

Lepus americanus

LENGTH:
head and body, 15-18½ in.; tail, 2 in.

WHAT TO LOOK FOR:
large hind feet; dark brown color (white in winter).

HABITAT:
northern and alpine forests, swamps, brushy areas.

Twice a year this whiskered mammal, also called the Varying Hare, changes its coat. Beginning in September the brown summer coat is gradually replaced by white-tipped hairs, a process lasting up to three months; the reverse process begins in March. The name Snowshoe Hare reflects another seasonal change—in autumn the animal develops dense fur pads on its feet. (The pads supply insulation and enhance mobility in snow.) Diet also changes with the seasons. When green plants are no longer available, the hare feeds on twigs and buds, leaving a characteristic slanted cut on the severed end of the branch. Like other hares and rabbits, it rests in thick cover during the day. Camouflaged by its color, it may reveal its whereabouts only by its tracks.

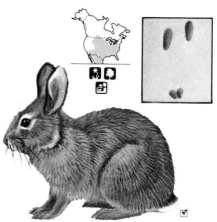

Eastern Cottontail

Sylvilagus floridanus

LENGTH:
head and body, 13½-16 in.; tail, 2 in.

WHAT TO LOOK FOR:
short-eared, short-tailed rabbit; white tail conspicuous when running.

HABITAT:
brushy areas, forest edges, swamps.

This rabbit flourishes almost everywhere east of the Rocky Mountains. (Other kinds of cottontails occur in the West.) Cats, foxes, hawks, and owls help to keep its numbers under some control; human hunters also take a heavy toll. But the rabbit's legendary fecundity means that the population is constantly being renewed. Each year a female cottontail produces several litters, each with up to seven young, and rabbits born in early spring may breed that very summer. Rabbits bear naked, blind young; hares (including the jackrabbits) are born furred and with their eyes open. Another difference is their gait; rabbits have shorter legs and are better suited for running.

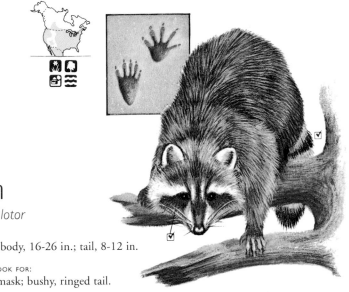

Raccoon

Procyon lotor

LENGTH:
head and body, 16-26 in.; tail, 8-12 in.

WHAT TO LOOK FOR:
dark eye mask; bushy, ringed tail.

HABITAT:
bottomlands, forested edges of streams, lakes; rocky cliffs near water.

Equally at home in suburban, rural, and forested areas, the wily Raccoon is unperturbed by the presence of man. Having learned to pry the lids from garbage cans, it makes regular nightly raids in certain locales, and will eat almost any type of food, including nuts, berries, grain, bird eggs, carrion, rodents, insects, and crayfish. According to popular myth, Raccoons wash everything they eat. Though in captivity they often dunk their food, this behavior is not related to cleanliness; instead, it is believed to reflect their natural habit of finding food in water. Raccoons mate in late winter and give birth to litters averaging four young in spring. Mother and young may remain together during the first winter. Raccoons do not hibernate but may be inactive for long periods during cold weather.

Ringtail (Cacomistle)

Bassariscus astutus

LENGTH:
head and body, 14-16 in.; tail, 14-15½ in.

WHAT TO LOOK FOR:
light-colored body; tail very long, bushy, ringed, tipped with black.

HABITAT:
rocky hills, cliffs, chaparral; usually near water.

The 2-pound Ringtail, smaller and more lithe than the Raccoon, is most at home in wooded and rocky areas of the southwestern states. This nocturnal hunter usually pounces from ambush and kills its prey (mainly birds and small mammals) with a bite on the neck. It was formerly kept in mines to control the rodent population—hence the alternative name of Miner's Cat. Ringtails are agile climbers and use their tails for balance. During the day they sometimes sleep high in trees, invisible except for their long, dangling tails. In the southern part of their range they are known as Cacomistles, a name derived from Indian words for "half" and "mountain lion."

Wolverine

Gulo gulo

LENGTH:
head and body, 28-34 in.; tail, 8-9½ in.

WHAT TO LOOK FOR:
dark fur; broad, yellowish bands on forehead and sides; bushy tail.

HABITAT:
high mountains, Arctic tundra.

This animal goes by a variety of names. As one, Skunk-bear, suggests, it looks like a cross between a skunk and a bear. (It is actually a member of the weasel family, as are the skunks.) The name Wolverine probably stems from its predatory nature. For an animal of its size, the Wolverine is exceptionally strong; under certain circumstances it can kill animals as large as a deer. It is a slow plodder but can cover long distances through the snow. Also called the Indian Devil, it raids traps and food caches and is a nuisance to trappers. It eats not only mammals but also fish, berries, and carcasses left by other predators. Not surprisingly, another of the Wolverine's names is Glutton.

Striped Skunk

Mephitis mephitis

LENGTH:
head and body, 15-19 in.; tail, 7-10 in.

WHAT TO LOOK FOR:
white facial stripe, neck patch, and V
on back; mottled bushy tail.

HABITAT:
open forests, farmlands, brushy areas,
prairies; usually near water.

When provoked, the Striped Skunk arches its
back, raises its tail, stamps its front feet, and
shuffles backward. If the warning is not heeded,
the animal ejects a fine spray of acrid, blinding
fluid from its anal glands. As a result, few animals
other than large owls prey on skunks. The Striped
Skunk ambles about at dusk and after nightfall in
search of animal and plant food. It is especially
fond of grasshoppers, ground beetles, and even
bees, excavating their nests and eating the larvae.
It becomes fat in autumn and spends the winter
in a den, emerging in warm weather to forage.

Spotted Skunk

Spilogale putorius

LENGTH:
head and body, 8-14 in.; tail, 5-9 in.

WHAT TO LOOK FOR:
variable black and white pattern, with white
spots on head and many stripes or spots on
body; white tip on bushy tail.

HABITAT:
open woods, brushy and rocky areas,
prairies; usually near water.

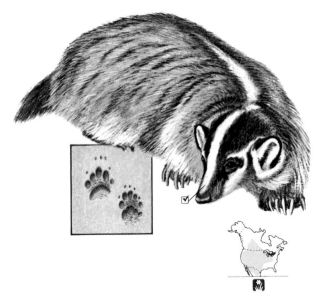

Badger

Taxidea taxus

LENGTH:
head and body, 18-23 in.; tail,
4½-6 in.

WHAT TO LOOK FOR:
flattened body; short legs;
shaggy fur; black facial pattern;
white stripe on top of head.

HABITAT:
dry, treeless areas.

A tenacious fighter, this heavy-bodied member of the weasel family has scent glands that emit a strong odor and long front claws capable of tearing flesh. The Badger is a remarkable burrower that can rapidly dig itself out of sight when danger threatens. Large holes dug as it pursues rodents are more likely to be seen than the animal itself, which is active mainly at night. Badgers are usually solitary except in late summer, during the breeding season. Though the word *badger* has come to mean *annoy*, this does not stem from the animal's scrappy disposition. Instead, it comes from badger-baiting, a former "sport" in which the European species was tormented by dogs.

◄ Spotted Skunk (AT LEFT) The Spotted Skunk's warning is a handstand; the animal puts its weight on its front feet, raises its hind-quarters into the air, and aims the openings of its scent glands at the source of provocation. The spray is even sharper and more acrid than the Striped Skunk's. It eats the same type of food but depends more on mammals (especially mice and rats) than its larger relative. The diets of both change with the seasons. A study of Spotted Skunks in Iowa found mammals to be the most important winter food. The proportion of insects increased in spring and summer, and fruits were eaten mainly in the fall.

Marten

Martes americana

LENGTH:
head and body, 13½-20 in.;
tail, 6½-9½ in.

WHAT TO LOOK FOR:
slender body; long, bushy tail; tail
and underparts darker than back;
buffy patch on throat and breast.

HABITAT:
coniferous forests, cedar swamps.

Usually a nighttime hunter, this
arboreal weasel is occasionally seen
during the day as it leaps and runs
along branches in pursuit of squirrels. It also feeds on other small
mammals, birds, insects, and berries.
Martens are solitary; the males are
quarrelsome and associate with females only in summer, during the mating season. Young martens are not
born until spring. Though this period of gestation may seem exceptionally
long, the embryos do not develop throughout the entire time. Instead, they
undergo a spurt of growth only during the month before birth. This phenomenon, called
delayed implantation, occurs in other mammals, including the Nine-banded Armadillo,
Black Bear, and Fisher (*Martes pennanti*), a large, all-dark relative of the Marten.

MARTEN

FISHER

Ermine

Mustela erminea

LENGTH:
head and body, 5-9½ in.;
tail, 2-4 in.

WHAT TO LOOK FOR:
long, slim body; tail black at
tip; summer fur dark brown
above, white below; winter fur
white except for tail tip.

HABITAT:
forests, brushy areas; usually
near water.

SUMMER

WINTER

Long-tailed Weasel
Mustela frenata

LENGTH:
head and body, 7½-15 in.; tail, 3½-7 in.

WHAT TO LOOK FOR:
long, slim body; tail black at tip; feet and legs brown; body brown above, pale below; yellowish white (except tip of tail) in winter in northern part of range.

HABITAT:
open country, forests, many other areas; usually near water.

Though larger and more powerful than the Ermine, the Long-tailed Weasel feeds primarily on the same type of prey. It also hunts birds, especially ground-nesters, and can cause considerable damage in a chicken coop. (It benefits humans, however, by killing rats and mice in fields and barns.) Like the Ermine, this weasel changes color twice a year, except in the southern pant of its range. Molting occurs during a period of about four weeks, and the gradual nature of the process explains the part-white, part-brown individuals that are sometimes encountered. Molts are triggered mainly by changes in day length, though temperature also plays a role.

◄ Ermine (AT LEFT) This ferocious little carnivore, also called the Short-tailed Weasel, is quick and agile. With a slender, almost serpentine body, it can easily move through small burrows in nocturnal pursuit of rodents. It also climbs well and chases squirrels and chipmunks into trees, usually killing them with a bite in the neck. Often the Ermine does not immediately eat all that it kills but returns to the carcass for several meals. Twice a year, in spring and fall, the Ermine changes color dramatically. The white winter pelts are luxury furs, usually obtained from animals trapped in Europe, Asia, and Canada.

Mink

Mustela vison

LENGTH:
head and body, 11½-20 in.; tail, 5-9 in.

WHAT TO LOOK FOR:
long, slim body; fur dark red-brown, except
for small pale area on chin and scattered white
spots on underside.

HABITAT:
along rivers, streams, and lakes; occasionally
in tidal marshes.

Mink never live far from water. They are excellent swimmers and prey on
both aquatic and terrestrial animals, including Muskrats, fishes, rabbits,
and snakes. The males are larger than the females and have a more extensive
hunting area. Mink are fierce and seemingly fearless fighters that scream,
spit, hiss, and—like other members of the weasel family (including skunks)—
emit a pungent odor when provoked. Adults are usually solitary except in the
breeding season. Mating occurs in winter (both sexes are polygamous), and
litters of 2 to 10 kits are born in spring. By early summer the young follow
their mother on hunting forays; by autumn they are able to fend for themselves. Though some Mink are still being trapped, ranch-raised individuals
supply most of the commercial market.

River Otter

Lutra canadensis

LENGTH:
head and body, 20-35 in.; tail, 10-18½ in.

WHAT TO LOOK FOR:
weasellike shape; dark brown fur, often with
golden gloss on head and shoulders; thick, furry
tail, tapering toward tip.

HABITAT:
rivers, streams, lakes, and neighboring areas;
occasionally in coastal waters.

otters sliding on snow

Otters truly seem to enjoy life. These sociable animals wrestle, play tag, slide down muddy or
snowy riverbanks, and roll about in grasses and reeds. They express themselves vocally through
chirps, whistles, growls, and screams. Although male and female stay together for part of the
year, the female drives her mate away before giving birth to a litter of two or three young in
early spring. Blind at birth but fully furred, the young grow slowly and do not venture out of
the den—a hollow log or a beaver or muskrat burrow—until they are 10 to 12 weeks old.
Then the mother begins teaching them to swim, dive, and hunt, aided by the father after the
young are about six months old. Though otters are mainly fish eaters, they also feed on frogs,
crayfish, and other small animals. Their streamlined bodies, webbed toes, and eyes and ears
that can be closed underwater make them well adapted to an aquatic life.

Red Fox

Vulpes vulpes

LENGTH:
head and body, 20-30 in.;
tail, 14-16 in.

WHAT TO LOOK FOR:
usually reddish on back and face,
white on underparts; tail bushy,
white-tipped; black legs and feet.

HABITAT:
farmlands; forests with open areas.

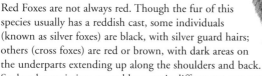

Red Foxes are not always red. Though the fur of this
species usually has a reddish cast, some individuals
(known as silver foxes) are black, with silver guard hairs;
others (cross foxes) are red or brown, with dark areas on
the underparts extending up along the shoulders and back.
Such color variation, caused by genetic differences, can occur even among pups in the same litter. Red Foxes are born in spring and weaned when one month old or more. Active throughout
the year, they are best observed in early morning and late afternoon. These notorious chicken
thieves are actually quite opportunistic in diet; although they prey mainly on small mammals
and birds, they also eat insects, carrion, and fruits.

Kit Fox

Vulpes velox

LENGH:
head and body, 14-22 in.;
tail, 9-11½ in.

WHAT TO LOOK FOR:
smaller than Red Fox; fur pale
rusty-gray, with white belly; black-
tipped tail; large ears.

HABITAT:
flat, open, sandy areas; deserts;
near pinyon pines.

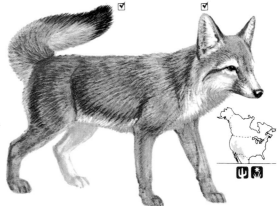

Gray Fox
Urocyon cinereoargenteus

LENGTH:
head and body, 22-30 in.;
tail, 10-15 in.

WHAT TO LOOK FOR:
coat coarse, salt-and-pepper
gray, with orange and white
markings; tail bushy, black-
tipped, with black stripe
on top.

HABITAT:
open woodlands, chaparral,
desert edges.

Foxes belong to the dog family
(*Canidae*), and canids are noticeably deficient in tree-climbing ability. But the Gray Fox is
unusual—it climbs trees readily by clasping the trunk with its front legs and pushing itself
up with its hind feet. Like other foxes, this grizzled animal uses ground burrows for
escape holes and birthing sites. Gray Foxes den in hollow logs, tree trunks, and rocks.

◀ Kit Fox (AT LEFT) The smallest fox in North America has exceptionally large ears, which are
believed to enhance its ability to detect rodents and other prey moving across the open
land. Like the Red Fox, this species mates in winter and often uses burrows excavated by
other mammals as maternity dens. Vixens (females) produce one litter a year, usually of
four or five pups. Although Kit Foxes may move about near their dens during the day,
these dainty animals are basically nighttime hunters. Poisoned bait intended for other
predators has caused their numbers to decline.

Coyote
Canis latrans

LENGTH:
head and body, 32-40 in.;
tail, 12-15 in.

WHAT TO LOOK FOR:
gray on back, with red on flanks;
tawny legs, feet, and ears; tail held
between legs when running.

HABITAT:
prairies, open forests, brush.

The Coyote's nocturnal serenades—a chorus of
howls, barks, and wails—epitomize the American
West. But Coyotes have drastically extended their
range and now commonly occur throughout the
U.S. They adapt well to the presence of man (even
to the extent of raiding garbage cans) and have
moved into areas extensively cleared for farming.
Frequently condemned as livestock-killers, they are
primarily predators on rodents, rabbits, and other
small animals. Occasionally several adults cooperate
in hunting large prey such as deer. Coyotes belong
to the dog family. They resemble German shepherds
and have been known to mate with domestic dogs.

Gray Wolf

Canis lupus

LENGTH:
head and body, 40 52 in.;
tail, 13-19 in.

WHAT TO LOOK FOR:
large doglike animal; fur usually
gray but varies from silvery white
to black.

HABITAT:
open forests, tundra.

Maligned through the ages as a vicious predator, the
wolf might better be admired for its complex social
organization. The wolf pack, usually numbering four
to seven individuals, is a society of parents, young,
and close relatives that follows a rigid hierarchy. The
leader, or alpha male, appears to control the pack's
activities and is often the only male to breed; usually
he is paired with the dominant female. Wolves have a
wide repertoire of social behavior, communicating by
posture, voice, and scent. They cooperate in feeding,
protecting, and training the pups. They are mainly
big-game hunters, preying on deer and other large
mammals, but will also attack smaller mammals and
birds. The Gray, or Timber, Wolf is native to both
North America and Eurasia; the rapidly disappearing
Red Wolf (*Canis rufus*) is strictly a resident of the
southeastern states.

Grizzly Bear

Ursus arctos horribilis

SIZE:
head and body length, 6-7 ft.;
shoulder height, 3-3½ ft.

WHAT TO LOOK FOR:
fur ranging from yellow to dark brown or black;
tips of hairs usually whitish (grizzled); hump on
shoulder; tail almost hidden in fur.

HABITAT:
mountain forests, tundra.

Lacking natural enemies, this giant does not always
conceal itself when disturbed but rears up on its
hind legs to get a better view of the situation. Like
its even larger relative, the Kodiak Bear (*Ursus arctos
middendorffi*), it can run as fast as a horse for short
distances. Although sometimes capable of killing
Moose and Caribou, it generally feeds on smaller
animals (such as rodents and fish) and on plant
material. It is dangerous to man only when
surprised, cornered, wounded, or with cubs.

Black Bear

Ursus americanus

SIZE:
head and body length, 4½-5
ft.; shoulder height, 2-3 ft.

WHAT TO LOOK FOR:
fur varying from cinnamon to
black; brown snout; no shoulder hump; small white breast
spot often present.

HABITAT:
forests, swamps, mountains.

Polar Bear
Ursus maritimus

SIZE:
head and body length, 6½-8 ft.;
shoulder height, 3-4 ft.

WHAT TO LOOK FOR:
yellowish-white fur.

HABITAT:
barren rocky shores, islands, ice floes.

With powerful shoulders, webbed paws,
streamlined bodies, and thick, oily fur, Polar
Bears are strong swimmers. But they are not
agile enough to catch swimming seals; they
either stalk basking individuals or wait for a
seal to surface at its breathing hole in the ice.
More carnivorous than other bears, Polar Bears
spend much of the year on and around ice floes.
In late summer, however, they come ashore and
forage for small animals, plants, and garbage. Pregnant females win-
ter and give birth in dens excavated in the snow; other individuals may den for shorter periods
of time. Churchill, Manitoba, is a prime area for seeing these massive creatures, which rival the
great Alaskan bears in size.

◄ **Black Bear** (AT LEFT) Omnivorous in diet, Black Bears feed on animals ranging in size from
insects to large mammals, as well as on plant material, carrion, and garbage. In autumn these
bears gain weight and retreat into dens under fallen trees, in caves, or in other protected areas.
There they sleep for several months, living off stored fat. Black Bears are not true hibernators;
their body temperature does not drop drastically, and occasionally they wake up and wander
away from their dens. Cubs are born about the end of January, while the sows (females) are
still in their dens. Bears produce exceptionally small offspring relative to adult size; a Black
Bear weighs about half a pound at birth, but a mature sow averages 300 pounds.

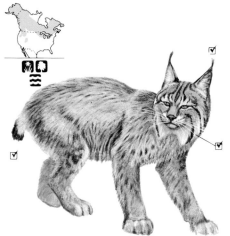

Lynx

Lynx lynx

LENGTH:
head and body, 30-38 in.; tail, 4 in.

WHAT TO LOOK FOR:
tufted ears; short, black-tipped tail; fur varied in color but usually grayish tan; scattered spots (more in summer); furry ruff.

HABITAT:
northern forests, swamps; occasionally on tundra.

This shy, elusive animal is an agile climber, swims well, and travels with ease among fallen timbers and moss-covered boulders. In winter its broad, well-furred feet act as snowshoes, allowing swift movement in deep snow. Lynx populations undergo ups and downs that closely follow those of its chief prey animal, the Varying (or Snowshoe) Hare. When hares are abundant (about every 10 years), the cats produce larger litters and their population increases. Eventually the hare population crashes, and a decline occurs in the number of Lynx. A similar relationship exists between owl and rodent populations, but the cycle recurs at shorter intervals.

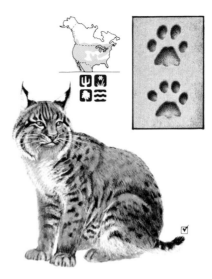

Bobcat

Lynx rufus

LENGTH:
head and body, 26-36 in.; tail, 5 in.

WHAT TO LOOK FOR:
tail short, black on top only; fur varies from dark
(forests) to light (open areas); spotted belly; spots
more conspicuous than on Lynx.

HABITAT:
canyon country, chaparral, forests, swamps.

The Bobcat is doing relatively well in the modern world. The commonest wild
feline in North America, it occurs in a variety of habitats, adapts well to the
presence of humans, and is increasing in number in some areas—all in sharp
contrast to the Lynx, a close relative with which it is often confused. Both Lynx
and Bobcats are essentially solitary animals with individual hunting ranges that
vary in size according to the availability of prey. (When prey is abundant, the cats
stay within a smaller area.) Though rabbits and hares are the Bobcat's usual food,
it will eat almost any mammal, reptile, or bird and has even been known to capture
bats roosting in caves. Caves, hollow logs, and rocky ledges are used as denning
sites by pregnant females. Kittens are usually born in spring, although females in
the southern part of the range may have a second litter later in the year.

Mountain Lion

Felis concolor

LENGTH:
head and body, 42-60 in.; tail, 24-36 in.

WHAT TO LOOK FOR:
fur tawny to gray, spotted only in young; small head; long, dark-tipped tail.

HABITAT:
mountains, forests, swamps, deserts.

Puma, Cougar, Panther, Painter, Catamount, Mountain Lion—all are names of the same creature, believed to be the most widely distributed carnivore in the New World. Usually solitary and nocturnal, the Mountain Lion hunts deer and other mammals by stalking and rushing or by pouncing from trees and overhanging rocks. Like other large cats, it often kills by biting the neck of its prey. Neck bites of a gentler sort also occur during mating. Although breeding may occur at any time of year, most births take place in summer. The spotted kittens nurse for five or six weeks, grow unspotted coats at about six months, and remain with the mother for as long as two years. This is one of the few cat species in which the adult's fur has no spots or stripes.

Mountain Sheep
Ovis canadensis

SIZE:
head and body length, 5-6 ft.; shoulder height, 2½-3½ ft.

WHAT TO LOOK FOR:
ram's horns massive, spiraling; ewe's horns much smaller, slightly curved; fur brown or grayish brown; whitish rump.

HABITAT:
rugged, sparsely wooded mountain slopes.

Also known as the Bighorn (its horns measure up to 4 feet), this heavy-bodied sheep has a remarkable capacity for climbing and jumping, thanks to the structure of its hooves. The halves of each hoof separate, so that the feet cling firmly to rocky terrain. The soles are soft and cushionlike, allowing the Bighorn to keep its balance as it moves across uneven or slippery ground. Mountain Sheep are gregarious animals. Groups of old rams roam together in summer, then separate to join bands of ewes and young in fall; they all move to lower valleys for the winter. Though in winter they may rely on willows and other woody plants, they are primarily grass-eating creatures.

Mountain Goat

Oreamnos americanus

SIZE:
head and body length, 5-5½ ft.; shoulder height, 3-3½ ft.

WHAT TO LOOK FOR:
fur white, long; horns black, curving backward; bearded chin.

HABITAT:
steep slopes, cliffs, woods; usually above timberline.

This sure-footed animal grazes well above the timberline, preferring steep mountainsides and cliffs to sheltered valleys. It generally moves quite slowly. But when danger threatens, it rapidly scales cliff faces, reaching nooks and crannies that are inaccessible to predators. Avalanches are a chief cause of death, though Mountain Lions, wolves, foxes, and eagles sometimes take young goats, or kids. Born in April or May, the kids are able to stand up only a few minutes after birth and can follow their mother over difficult terrain within several days.

Pronghorn
Antilocapra americana

SIZE:
head and body length, 4-4½ ft.; shoulder height, 3-3½ ft.

WHAT TO LOOK FOR:
fur tan, white on belly and rump; 2 white stripes on breast; horns slightly curved, with single forward-projecting prong.

HABITAT:
prairies, sagebrush flats.

North America's swiftest mammal, sometimes called an antelope, can reach speeds of more than 40 miles an hour, cover 20 feet in one leap, and outdistance nearly all predators. Adapted to the temperature extremes of the open plains, it maintains a constant body temperature by adjusting its loose, hollow-haired fur. When the hairs lie flat, cold air is kept out; when hairs are erect, air circulates near the skin and allows body heat to escape. In dangerous situations, and also during courtship, it signals to other Pronghorns by raising the white hairs on its rump. Pronghorns are the only animals that shed the outer part of their horns once a year.

Wapiti (Elk)

Cervus elaphus

SIZE:
head and body length, 7½-9½ ft.; tail length,
4½-8 in.; shoulder height, 4-5 ft.

WHAT TO LOOK FOR:
large size; huge antlers (males); red-brown fur;
pale rump; short tail.

HABITAT:
mountain meadows, forested
areas, lakeshores; valleys,
grassland edges (winter).

Wapiti is an Indian word for "white," a reference to the light rump color of this gregarious deer. Though Wapiti are less common today than in the past (they formerly roamed even the eastern states), herds are widely distributed in mountain forests and adjacent valleys of the West. In summer Wapiti cows and calves graze together in groups; bulls form separate herds. In autumn the bulls' loud, resonant bugling announces the rut, or mating season, when they fight (sometimes to the death) for possession of a harem. Males and females forage together in winter, then separate for the birth of the young. The calves have spotted fur, unlike Moose and Caribou calves.

Moose

Alces alces

SIZE:
head and body length,
7½-10 ft.; tail length,
2½-3½ in.; shoulder
height, 5-6½ ft.

WHAT TO LOOK FOR:
large size; antlers
(males) massive, flattened,
pronged; fleshy dewlap on throat;
upper lip overhangs lower.

HABITAT:
northern forests; often around freshwater.

Moose are the largest members of the deer family; males in autumn may weigh more than
a thousand pounds. Standing or swimming in lakes and ponds, they feed on many kinds
of aquatic plants. Moose are not highly social animals; they are solitary or associate in
small groups most of the year. In the fall the males become restless and aggressive, engag-
ing in antler-to-antler combat and searching for a series of mates. Calves (often twins) are
born in spring. Weak at birth, these gangling, unspotted creatures remain hidden and
inactive for several days. Wolves and bears prey on the calves, as they also do on the aged
and weak, but few predators can successfully challenge a healthy adult. Moose swim well
and run easily through the snow, and they possess formidable weapons in their legs and
hooves. Males shed their antlers in winter and begin to grow them again in spring.

White-tailed Deer

Odocoileus virginianus

SIZE:
head and body length, 4-6 ft; tail length, 7-11 in.;
shoulder height, 2¾-3½ ft.

WHAT TO LOOK FOR:
tail white on underside, raised when alarmed;
antlers (males) have main beam with several prongs;
fur reddish (summer) or grayish brown (winter).

HABITAT:
forests, swamps, adjacent brushy areas.

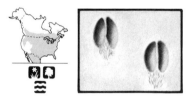

The cutting of forests and clearing of land for farming have favored these graceful deer, now the most abundant hoofed mammals in North America. Early morning and dusk are the best times to see them; at other times of day they usually rest and digest their food. Except in winter, they are not gregarious and seldom appear in groups of more than three animals (a doe and two fawns). Females normally have no antlers. Males begin growing them several months after birth, shed them each winter, and develop them anew each spring and summer. The age of a deer cannot be told by the size of the antlers or the number of points (tines), for antler development is determined by nutrition, not age.

Mule Deer
Odocoileus hemionus

SIZE:
head and body length, 4½-6½ ft.; tail length, 4½-9 in.; shoulder height, 3-3½ ft.

WHAT TO LOOK FOR:
tail black-tipped or all black on top ("Black-tailed Deer"); antlers (males) fork into 2 nearly equal branches; fur reddish brown (summer) or grayish (winter); large ears.

HABITAT:
mountain forests, wooded hills and valleys, chaparral, brushy deserts.

Unlike the White-tailed Deer, the Mule Deer (named for its large, mulelike ears) avoids areas of human activity. On summer evenings single individuals or groups of Mule Deer can be seen near forest edges in western parks; in winter large, loosely structured herds assemble on brushy slopes in the foothills where browse (the twigs and buds of woody plants) is available. The animals move to higher elevations in spring. Like other deer, this species ruts in autumn, when males contest for and associate briefly with the females. Spotted fawns, usually twins, are born in spring and weaned at about six weeks of age. Young females may stay with their mother for two years, but males leave in their first year.

Caribou

Rangifer tarandus

SIZE:
head and body length, 5½-7½ ft.;
tail length, 4-5½ in.; shoulder height, 3½-4 ft.

WHAT TO LOOK FOR:
stocky body; antlers branching into 3 slightly flattened tines,
one extending over brow; white neck, rump, and "socks."

HABITAT:
northern forests, bogs, tundra.

Unlike other deer, Caribou of both sexes usually have antlers, although the males' far surpass those of the females. The Caribou has another peculiarity—as it moves, a tendon in its foot rubs against a bone and produces an audible click. The sound becomes especially noticeable when the animals move in great numbers, as they do during the migration of the tundra-dwelling race (known as the Barren-ground Caribou). Sometimes considered a separate species, the tundra animals winter in the scattered spruce-fir forests south of their summer range. Although 100,000 animals may band together just before migration, the typical herd is much smaller and relatively homogeneous in age and sex. The Reindeer of the Old World are considered by many to belong to the same species as the American Caribou.

Bison

Bison bison

SIZE:
head and body length, 7-11½ ft.; tail length, 20-26 in.;
shoulder height, 5-6 ft.

WHAT TO LOOK FOR:
large head; shoulder hump; horns on sides of head; long,
shaggy fur on shoulders and front legs.

HABITAT:
prairies; open woodlands in north.

Bison once grazed the continent from the mountain grasslands of the West as far east as
Georgia. Hunted nearly to extinction by the end of the 19th century, these shaggy creatures
were bred in zoos and on ranches and then released in parks and refuges. Today they can be
seen in such areas as Yellowstone National Park (Wyoming), Wood Buffalo National Park
(Alberta), and the National Bison Range (Montana). Often called Buffalo, they belong to
the same family as sheep, goats, and cattle. All have horns with a bony core that are retained
from year to year. Bison travel in bands commonly numbering 60 or more but occasionally
form larger herds. Calves follow their mothers closely for two to three weeks after birth,
then often band together in playful nursery groups. Weaned at about seven months, they
feed on a variety of green plants for the rest of their lives. Bison have been known to produce calves at 30 years of age.

Northern Fur Seal

Callorhinus ursinus

LENGTH:
4½-6½ ft.

WHAT TO LOOK FOR:
blackish above, reddish below; brown face;
gray shoulders; small, pointed ears.

HABITAT:
cold seas; comes ashore only for breeding.

The Northern Fur Seal, valued
for its lustrous pelt, breeds on
three groups of islands in and
around the North Pacific. The
largest herd is found on the Pribilof
Islands, off the Alaskan coast. After a winter at sea
the mature bulls (harem masters) arrive on the beaches in late spring. Then come the females,
which give birth shortly after arrival and then mate; offspring from these matings will be born
the following year. After suckling their young for about a week, the females leave for a week or
so at sea. They hunt fish and squid, return to nurse their pups for a day, and maintain this
schedule until the young are weaned. In autumn the bulls, weakened by constant fighting and
lack of food (they do not eat during the breeding season), are the first to depart. In winter the
seals may swim as far south as southern California—a journey of several thousand miles.

California Sea Lion
Zalophus californianus

LENGTH:
6-8 ft.

WHAT TO LOOK FOR:
brown fur (blackish when wet); high forehead; small, pointed ears; animal barks frequently.

HABITAT:
rocky coasts, surf, open sea.

Although the names "sea lion" and "seal" are often used interchangeably, the animals are not the same. There are two major differences: sea lions, and also fur seals, have visible, external ears, and they can turn their flippers forward when walking on land. The trained "seals" of circuses, zoos, and aquariums are usually California Sea Lions. In their natural habitat these graceful swimmers ride the surf, leap in and out of the water, and playfully cavort near shore. They spend much of the day basking on land and are believed to feed mainly at night on a typically seallike diet of mollusks and fish. The Northern, or Steller, Sea Lion (*Eumetopias jubatus*) is a larger creature with lighter-colored fur.

Sea Otter

Enhydra lutris

LENGTH:
head and body, 29-39 in.;
tail, 9½-12 in.

WHAT TO LOOK FOR:
fur glossy, blackish brown, with white-tipped
hairs; head area lighter in color; webbed,
flipperlike feet.

HABITAT:
kelp beds along rocky shores.

The Sea Otter is the smallest marine mammal. Almost wholly aquatic, it comes ashore only
in severe storms. In water it propels itself by alternate strokes of the broad hind feet, spending
much of the time backstroking, with its head above the surface. The Sea Otter feeds in relatively shallow water, searching the bottom for abalone and also preying on squid, octopus,
and sea urchins. It carries food to the surface, uses its belly as a table as it floats on its back,
and cracks shells by placing a flat rock on its chest and hitting them against the rock.

Harbor Seal

Phoca vitulina

LENGTH:
4½-5½ ft.

WHAT TO LOOK FOR:
fur varying in color (dark gray
with brown spots, dark brown
with gray spots, all gray, or all brown);
no visible ears.

HABITAT:
coastal waters, estuaries, harbors; occasionally in lakes.

Few seals spend as much time ashore as this common species, which is believed to have the
widest range of any seal. Harbor Seals wait out low tide on the beach and normally take to the
water only as the tide comes in, sometimes following the tidal flow far into an estuary as they
fish. Like elephant seals, they submerge by slipping beneath the surface; in contrast, fur seals
and sea lions arch their backs, thrust forward, and dive. Harbor Seals can reach depths of 300
feet and stay underwater for nearly half an hour. They mate both in water and on land and on
occasion have been known to give birth in the sea. Birth normally occurs on sandbars, ledges,
offshore islands, or ice floes.

Northern Elephant Seal
Mirounga angustirostris

LENGTH:
males to 20 ft., females to 11 ft.

WHAT TO LOOK FOR:
large size; skin brown to grayish, nearly hairless; snout flabby, overhanging on old males; ears not visible.

HABITAT:
sandy beaches, warm waters.

This seal takes its name from its great size and overhanging snout. Bulls weigh several tons; when alarmed or defending their harems, they bellow through and inflate their snouts. Usually rather lethargic, Northern Elephant Seals were easy victims for 19th-century hunters who sought their blubber as a source of oil. Only one small colony, on an island off the coast of Baja California, remained by the 1890s. Protected by Mexico since 1911, Northern Elephant Seals have made a remarkable recovery; they now number more than 10,000 and have extended their range up the Pacific coast to San Francisco.

Manatee

Trichechus manatus

LENGTH:
7½-12½ ft.

WHAT TO LOOK FOR:
bulky body; lips cleft in center, covered with bristles; no rear flippers; tail flattened, rounded at tip.

HABITAT:
shallow lagoons, estuaries, coastal rivers; usually in brackish water.

Although this odd-looking creature occasionally noses onto a riverbank to graze, it never comes completely ashore. Water is its home, but like all other mammals, it must have air to breathe. Manatees are born underwater. Immediately after birth, the mother brings the calf to the surface and is said to dunk it repeatedly until it can submerge on its own. To nurse, she holds the calf against her breast with her flippers. Manatees are rare animals, with a total estimated population of about 1,000. The best places to look for them are weed beds and, in winter, the warm outflow from power plants.

Common Dolphin

Delphinus delphis

LENGTH:
6½-8½ ft.

WHAT TO LOOK FOR:
black back and flippers; sides yellowish, blending to white below;
2 white lines between beak and forehead.

HABITAT:
temperate to warm seas; occasionally near shore.

With superb grace and showmanship, a school of Common Dolphins will
frolic about the bow of a moving ship and leap in unison above the sea.
Within a group there appears to be a well-defined social structure, with
mature males dominant over all others. Not a deep diver, this species usually
swims near the surface, breathing every 30 seconds and feeding on the typical
toothed-whale diet of fish and squid. Dolphins and porpoises are small
relatives of whales and can be distinguished from one another by the shape of
their snouts. Dolphin snouts are beaked or bottle-nosed; porpoises' are blunt.
There is also a fish called the Dolphin, which has a porpoiselike snout.

Harbor Porpoise
Phocoena phocoena

LENGTH:
4-6 ft.

WHAT TO LOOK FOR:
blunt nose; black back; pink sides; white belly; black line from
mouth to flipper; triangular dorsal fin.

HABITAT:
along Atlantic and Pacific coasts; harbors; occasionally in rivers.

Traveling in pairs or larger groups, Harbor Porpoises cruise just below the surface and rise
to breathe about four times a minute. Like whales, dolphins and porpoises take in and
expel air through blowholes near the top of the head. (Dolphins, porpoises, and toothed
whales have single blowholes; baleen whales have two.) Although the Harbor Porpoise is
not as playful as some of its relatives, the male and female swim together, touch, and
vocalize in an elaborate courtship. A single calf is born after a year's gestation.

Whales and their kin.

Dolphins and porpoises are essentially small versions of whales. All
members of the group of mammals known as cetaceans, they have
certain features in common:

- They are strictly aquatic, remaining in water even to breed.
- They are relatively large. Even the smallest species grows to lengths
  of 5 feet or more.
- The front limbs are paddlelike flippers. Hind limbs are not visible.
- The tails are flattened horizontally and notched in the center. Each
  half of the tail is called a fluke.
- Hair is absent except for a few bristles around the mouth.

Bottle-nosed Dolphin

Tursiops truncatus

LENGTH:
9-12 ft.

WHAT TO LOOK FOR:
short projecting snout; grayish above, somewhat
paler below.

HABITAT:
along Atlantic and Pacific coasts.

The playfulness, friendliness, and intelligence of the Bottle-nosed Dolphin have
won it fame as a star performer in marine aquariums and films. This especially
vocal animal emits complicated whistles and chirps as it communicates with
others of its kind. Like all toothed whales, it also sends out ultrasonic signals
that help it navigate and locate prey. (This technique, also used by bats, is
called echolocation or sonar.) Friendly toward man, it turns fierce when its
young are menaced by sharks. One or more individuals have been observed
repeatedly ramming an attacking fish at high speed until the molester was
killed. This is the commonest dolphin along the Atlantic shore; a close relative,
Gill's Bottle-nosed Dolphin (*Tursiops gillii*), lives in the Pacific.

Killer Whale

Orcinus orca

LENGTH:
15-30 ft.

WHAT TO LOOK FOR:
large, high dorsal fin; black and white pattern.

HABITAT:
Pacific and Atlantic waters; often near shore.

◀ Killer Whale (AT LEFT) Weighing up to 20,000 pounds, Killer Whales, or Orcas, are formidable predators. They slice through the water at a top speed of 30 knots. They pursue their prey in packs of up to 50 individuals, swimming in close formation and often leaping and diving in unison. A pack will herd a school of tuna or salmon into a cove, where the fish are easier to catch. Killer Whales are the only whales to prey frequently on warm-blooded animals (mammals and birds). They will surround even a large whale and tear away chunks of flesh with knife-like teeth. In Antarctic waters they capture penguins and seals by crashing through ice floes and dislodging their victims. In spite of their fearsome reputation, they have never been known to attack man. The Killer Whale is one of the easiest whales to identify—not only by species, but even by sex. Males are longer than females and have larger, more triangular fins.

Identifying whales.

Those lucky enough to spot a whale rarely see the entire animal. Whales come to the surface mainly to breathe, and for this only their blowholes need be exposed.

• Knowing which species are likely to be in the area helps to narrow down the possibilities. So does estimating the size of the whale. Keep in mind, however, that species overlap in size; a large Fin Whale and a small Blue Whale may be about the same size.

• Look at the color of the whale and the pattern of light and dark. Does the whale have a dorsal (back) fin? If so, note its shape. And if possible, note the shape of the head.

• Especially from a distance, the spout (shape, angle, and height) furnishes important clues.

Gray Whale
Eschrichtius robustus.

LENGTH:
to 45 ft.

WHAT TO LOOK FOR:
gray to nearly black, with blotches; no back fin;
spout relatively low (to 10 ft.) and rapid.

HABITAT:
breeds off Baja California; summers to the north,
frequently in large groups.

To the delight of crowds of whale watchers, Gray Whales often
swim only a few hundred yards offshore as they pass San Diego,
California, each year in early spring. They summer 5,000 miles to
the north (in the Bering and Chukchi seas) and return in late fall
on their way southward to the sheltered breeding lagoons of Baja
California. Gray Whales feed neither while breeding nor while
migrating. At other times they eat in shallow waters, unlike other
baleen whales, and frequently surface covered with mud. Another unusual
behavior is spyhopping—pushing their heads out of the water, probably to
look around. Once nearly extinct, this species has shown a marked increase in
number since protection was established in the 1930s.

Humpbacked Whale
Megaptera novaeangliae

LENGTH:
to 50 ft.

WHAT TO LOOK FOR:
blackish on back; white throat, chest, and undersides of flippers and tail; very long flippers; fan-shaped spout extends to 15 ft.

HABITAT:
ocean; occasionally just offshore, especially along Pacific coast.

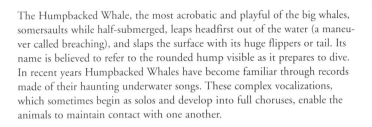

The Humpbacked Whale, the most acrobatic and playful of the big whales, somersaults while half-submerged, leaps headfirst out of the water (a maneuver called breaching), and slaps the surface with its huge flippers or tail. Its name is believed to refer to the rounded hump visible as it prepares to dive. In recent years Humpbacked Whales have become familiar through records made of their haunting underwater songs. These complex vocalizations, which sometimes begin as solos and develop into full choruses, enable the animals to maintain contact with one another.

Sperm Whale
Physeter catodon

LENGTH:
to 60 ft.

WHAT TO LOOK FOR:
square snout; huge head; lower jaw small, narrow; no back fin; spout angles forward.

HABITAT:
open ocean.

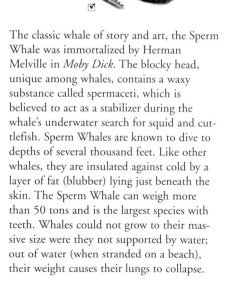

The classic whale of story and art, the Sperm Whale was immortalized by Herman Melville in *Moby Dick*. The blocky head, unique among whales, contains a waxy substance called spermaceti, which is believed to act as a stabilizer during the whale's underwater search for squid and cuttlefish. Sperm Whales are known to dive to depths of several thousand feet. Like other whales, they are insulated against cold by a layer of fat (blubber) lying just beneath the skin. The Sperm Whale can weigh more than 50 tons and is the largest species with teeth. Whales could not grow to their massive size were they not supported by water; out of water (when stranded on a beach), their weight causes their lungs to collapse.

Fin Whale

Balaenoptera physalus

LENGTH:
to 80 ft.

WHAT TO LOOK FOR:
grayish above, white below; dorsal fin small, toward rear
of body; fan-shaped spout extends to 20 ft.

HABITAT:
Atlantic Ocean south to Caribbean Sea; Pacific Ocean
south to Baja California.

Finbacks belong to the group of whales known as rorquals and
are characterized by deep grooves in their throats.
All rorquals, as well as the Gray and the
Humpbacked Whale, lack teeth. Instead, they
have strips of a hard, flexible substance called
baleen (or whalebone) that hang from the upper
jaw and act as a sieve. To feed, they gulp mouth-
fuls of water, close their jaws, and force water
out through the baleen plates. The fringed edges of the baleen
retain food organisms—usually tiny shrimplike animals called
krill. In summer, whale food is most abundant in Arctic and
Antarctic waters. Twice a year, therefore, baleen whales migrate
between polar feeding grounds and breeding grounds nearer the
Equator. The Blue Whale (*Balaenoptera musculus*), a baleen
whale with a more mottled appearance than the Fin Whale, is
the largest animal that has ever lived on earth.

Lizards, snakes, turtles, and alligators are all reptiles, despite their differences in shape, mobility, and way of life. The typical reptile has protective scales or plates, five clawed toes on each foot, and lungs instead of gills. Most species eat animals and lay eggs, but no single trait separates reptiles from other animals, as feathers do for birds.

Reptiles live just about everywhere in the United States and southern Canada—in freshwater, saltwater, forests, grasslands, deserts, and suburban places.

Alligators and Crocodiles
Found in the southeastern United States, these armored reptiles are most easily seen in southern Florida, especially in portions of Everglades National Park. There, from elevated boardwalks, you can observe enormous alligators as they bask on muddy banks or drift in the water like logs.

Turtles
Just under 50 species of turtles live in Canada and the United States, with Florida an especially turtle-rich state. These reptiles are most often found in or near water, especially on logs that are partially submerged.

A turtle carries its house on its back. The characteristic bony shell—the upper part is the carapace and the lower the plastron—is covered with hard shields, known as scutes. Soft-shelled turtles spend little time on land and often have reduced shells.

To identify a turtle, you may have to look at its plastron. Although turtles are toothless, they can inflict a painful bite, and should be handled with care—or in the case of the bigger ones, not at all.

Lizards
Although only a small number of the world's lizard species (some 115 out of 3,000) live north of the Mexican border, it is hard to imagine a more diverse group. Most have four legs, but the glass and the legless lizards have none at all. Bodies range from slim to massive; tails may be long and slender or short

and thick; scales may be smooth or spiny, with scale size as well as texture significant, since it may vary with region, age, and sex. In certain species the males are brighter in color, and they may be larger and longer-tailed than the females.

Lizards love sunshine, and most are active during the day. Look for little ones basking on stone walls, running along rail fences and logs, hiding in brush piles and heaps of dead leaves; inspect deserted buildings, sawdust piles, rocky slopes, canyon walls, and patches of sandy soil. Only one species in our region, the Gila Monster, is venomous (though others may bite), and the Gila is one lizard that many people would avoid on the basis of size alone.

Snakes

The human fascination with snakes can to some extent be explained by certain aspects of their biology and behavior. Snakes have no legs (although the Rubber Boa and closely related species have short remnants, known as spurs). They have no eyelids (hence the "unwinking stare"). They rely solely on animals for food (all other groups of reptiles include some plant-eating species). And they can injure and kill human beings.

Snakes often catch our attention only when they slither away from us. A deliberate search for these animals involves turning over logs and boards, poking through brush piles, and exploring rocky ledges, stone walls, and edges of ponds and streams. Do this with care; don't put your hand where you cannot see, or step over a log or a rock without first checking for snakes on the other side. Occasionally you may encounter not the snakes themselves but their cast-off skins (snakes molt several times a year).

A snake should never be handled unless you are absolutely certain it is not a venomous one. (Even nonvenomous ones, however, may bite.) Although only about a sixth of North America's 115 species are venomous, nearly all parts of the United States and southern Canada have at least one species that is. This book does not picture all of the venomous species, nor are all races and color variations of each species shown. Act with discretion in places where there may be snakes, and especially around the snakes themselves.

Alligator Snapping Turtles *Macroclemys*

Weighing up to 200 pounds or more, the Alligator Snapper is the world's largest fresh-water turtle. More sedentary than its relative the Snapping Turtle, it lies submerged and half buried in the mud, wiggling the pink wormlike projection on its tongue. When a fish is lured by the "bait," the turtle's jaws snap shut. (Turtles are toothless but have sharp edges on their jaws.) The hefty reptile also feeds on worms, snails, mussels, carrion, and other kinds of turtles.

Alligator Snapping Turtle

Macroclemys temmincki

SHELL LENGTH:
13-26 in.

WHAT TO LOOK FOR:
carapace brown or gray, with 3 knobby ridges; head big, with strongly hooked beak; long tail.

HABITAT:
lakes, sloughs, deep rivers.

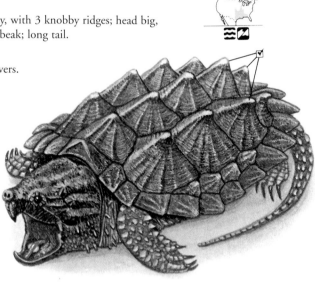

American Alligator

Alligator mississippiensis

LENGTH:
6-15 ft.

WHAT TO LOOK FOR:
snout broad, rounded; old adults gray-black; young black, with yellow crossbands.

HABITAT:
freshwater, brackish marshes, swamps, rivers, bayous.

Alligators *Alligator*

The largest reptiles in North America are also the loudest, the males bellowing lustily during the spring mating season. For a reptile, the female is an extraordinary parent. After mating she builds a nesting mound near water, lays 20 to 60 eggs, covers them with vegetation, and guards them until they hatch, some 10 weeks later. The young may stay with her for a year or more, eating frogs, crustaceans, and aquatic insects; adults prey on fish, turtles, birds, and small mammals. The alligator's close relative, the slender-snouted American Crocodile (*Crocodylus acutus*), is a rare resident of brackish and saltwater swamps in southern Florida.

Snapping Turtles *Chelydra*

The head and limbs of the Snapping Turtle are so large and its lower shell so small that the animal cannot retreat completely into its shell. Its powerful jaws are its defense. Opportunistic feeders, Snappers eat a wide variety of aquatic plants and animals. They are usually seen floating lazily just below the water's surface. Females occasionally come on land to seek out sites for laying their eggs, and can be very aggressive at that time.

Snapping Turtle

Chelydra serpentina

SHELL LENGTH:
8-20 in.

WHAT TO LOOK FOR:
head big, with powerful jaws; carapace brown, often covered with algae or mud; long tail.

HABITAT:
quiet mud-bottomed waters.

Musk Turtles *Sternotherus*

When annoyed, these small turtles secrete a foul-smelling yellowish fluid, as do the closely related mud turtles. Many of their habits are similar, too. Both prowl the bottom in search of small animal prey, occasionally annoying fishermen by robbing them of their bait. When handled, musk turtles and some mud turtles will attempt to bite. In spring they bask in the sun in shallow water or among floating plants, with only the top of the "dome" protruding above the surface. Sunbathing raises the temperature of turtles and other cold-blooded animals, speeding up their metabolism.

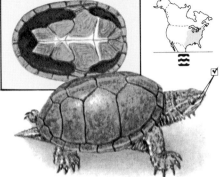

PLASTRON

Stinkpot (Musk Turtle)

Sternotherus odoratus

SHELL LENGTH:
3-5½ in.

WHAT TO LOOK FOR:
2 pale stripes on each side of head; carapace smooth, high-domed; plastron with 11 plates.

HABITAT:
streams, bayous, ponds, canals.

Loggerhead Musk Turtle

Sternotherus minor

SHELL LENGTH:
3-5¼ in.

WHAT TO LOOK FOR:
carapace brown or orange, often with dark border and dashes or streaks; plastron pink or yellow, with 11 plates.

HABITAT:
streams, rivers, sinkholes.

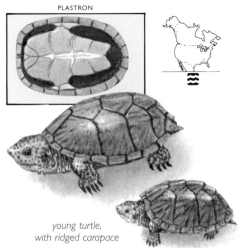

PLASTRON

young turtle, with ridged carapace

Mud Turtles *Kinosternon*

Although these turtles look like musk turtles from above, they are quite distinct when viewed from below. A mud turtle's plastron, or lower shell, covers most of its undersurface and bears two readily visible hinges. The hinges allow the turtle to bend its plastron when it pulls in its head, feet, and tail, thus furnishing added protection for its soft parts. In contrast, a musk turtle has a relatively small plastron with a single inconspicuous hinge.

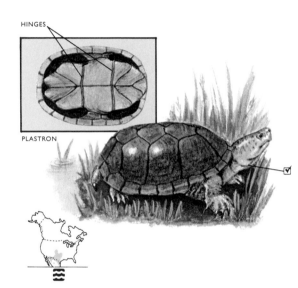

HINGES

PLASTRON

Yellow Mud Turtle

Kinosternon flavescens

SHELL LENGTH:
3½-6 in.

WHAT TO LOOK FOR:
carapace smooth, with dark-edged olive to brown plates; plastron yellow to brown, with 11 plates, 2 hinges, and dark seams; jaws and throat white or yellow.

HABITAT:
streams, rivers, ponds, lakes.

Eastern Mud Turtle

Kinosternon subrubrum

SHELL LENGTH:
3-3¾ in.

WHAT TO LOOK FOR:
carapace smooth, unmarked, olive
to dark brown; plastron yellow to
brown, with 11 plates and 2 hinges.

HABITAT:
lakes, swamps, salt marshes,
flooded ditches.

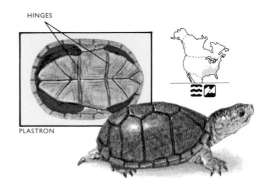

HINGES

PLASTRON

Diamondback Terrapins *Malaclemys*

Male and female Diamondback Terrapins differ greatly in size; the female may
be twice as long as her mate. (Map turtles exhibit this same trait.) The male's
longer, thicker tail and concave plastron facilitate mating. The female deposits 4
to 18 eggs above the high-tide line, in a cavity dug by her hind feet and filled
in with sand. The eggs hatch in two to four months, their numbers depleted
by marauding Raccoons, skunks, foxes, and gulls.

Diamondback Terrapin

Malaclemys terrapin

SHELL LENGTH:
4-9½ in.

WHAT TO LOOK FOR:
carapace gray to black, often with deeply
incised rings; head and neck gray, with
black flecks.

HABITAT:
salt marshes, estuaries.

Pond Turtles *Clemmys*

All of North America's four kinds of pond turtle spend some time on land. Although the Wood Turtle winters in a sheltered spot under water, at other times of year it may wander through woodlands, meadows, and plowed fields. The Spotted Turtle likes to bask on grassy tussocks in spring. "Spotties" also congregate on partially submerged logs, diving into the water when frightened and digging into the muddy bottom. The Western Pond Turtle, the only freshwater turtle in most of its range (it overlaps slightly with the Painted Turtle), is the most aquatic member of this group. Often seen basking alone on a favorite rock, log, or mudbank, it too is quick to dive when disturbed. The fourth pond turtle, the 4-inch Bog Turtle (*Clemmys muhlenbergi*), lives in scattered areas from New York to North Carolina. Bright yellow or orange blotches on the sides of its head contrast sharply with its basically brown shell. Like the other pond turtles, it feeds on mollusks and other small animals as well as on aquatic plants.

Wood Turtle

Clemmys insculpta

SHELL LENGTH:
5-9 in.

WHAT TO LOOK FOR:
carapace brown, with pyramidlike plates; plastron yellow, with black markings; neck and front legs often orange.

HABITAT:
woodland streams, farmlands, swamps, marshes.

PLASTRON

Spotted Turtle
Clemmys guttata

SHELL LENGTH:
3½-5 in.

WHAT TO LOOK FOR:
carapace black with yellowish spots; eyes brown (male) or orange (female).

HABITAT:
flooded woodlands, soft-bottomed streams, wet meadows, beaver ponds.

Western Pond Turtle
Clemmys marmorata

SHELL LENGTH:
3½-7 in.

WHAT TO LOOK FOR:
carapace smooth, flattened, olive to dark brown, usually with dark lines or spots that radiate from plate centers.

HABITAT:
still and slow-moving water, including reservoirs; sometimes in brackish water.

Box Turtles *Terrapene*

Although most kinds of turtles can withdraw into their shells, a box turtle can close up more completely than other species; because its plastron, or lower shell, is hinged, the front and rear sections can be bent upward so that the edges of the two shells meet. Box turtles are basically land-dwelling reptiles, but sometimes cool themselves in woodland pools or puddles. They are renowned for their longevity. Although some individuals have reportedly lived for more than a hundred years, estimates of a turtle's age are not always reliable. Dates scratched into the shell indicate little more than the personality of the person doing the carving. Counting the growth rings that develop on the plates overlying the shell can also be misleading. The rings do not develop equally each year, and after 10 or 15 years they may largely disappear.

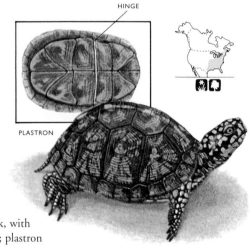

HINGE

PLASTRON

Eastern Box Turtle

Terrapene carolina

SHELL LENGTH:
4-8½ in.

WHAT TO LOOK FOR:
carapace high-domed, brown to black, with yellow, orange, or olive lines or spots; plastron plain or blotched, with hinge.

HABITAT:
damp forests, fields, and floodplains.

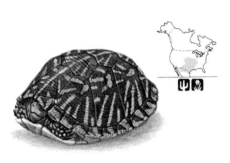

Western Box Turtle

Terrapene ornata

SHELL LENGTH:
4-5¾ in.

WHAT TO LOOK FOR:
carapace high-domed, black or brown, with radiating yellow lines; plastron hinged, similarly colored.

HABITAT:
dry prairies, scrub plains, woodlands, mesquite grasslands.

Chicken Turtles *Deirochelys*

A turtle's place in the food chain changes with age. Many of the aquatic species, including the Chicken Turtle, feed on small animals early in life and then switch to a vegetarian diet. As a turtle grows, its enemies also change. Young Chicken Turtles are eaten by Raccoons, otters, and wading birds; alligators and humans feed on the adults. (The succulent flesh of the Chicken Turtle was once marketed as food.) The larger species of turtle, such as the tortoises and snappers, have few predators except humans.

Chicken Turtle

Deirochelys reticularia

SHELL LENGTH:
4-10 in.

WHAT TO LOOK FOR:
neck unusually long, with yellow stripes; carapace with fine incised lines, giving wrinkled look.

HABITAT:
swamps; shallow, weedy ponds and lakes.

Map Turtles *Graptemys*

The dozen or so species of map turtle, all native to eastern North America, have a low ridge, or keel, along the midline of the carapace. Certain species, such as the False Map Turtle, have knobs on the keel and are sometimes called sawbacks. As the turtle ages, the knobs tend to wear down. The Ouachita Map Turtle (*Graptemys ouachitensis*), similar in appearance to the False Map Turtle and overlapping much of its range, is distinguished by four large yellow spots or alternating yellow and dark green bars on the underside of the head. Other map turtles are specific to certain river basins in the South. All are gregarious, basking together atop logs or on steep banks and vanishing quickly when an intruder appears. Although some species eat plants, invertebrates make up most of their diet. The female Map Turtle takes freshwater clams and snails, while the smaller male feeds on insects and crayfish.

Map Turtle

Graptemys geographica

SHELL LENGTH:
4-10¾ in.

WHAT TO LOOK FOR:
low central ridge on carapace; carapace greenish, with thin yellow-orange rings; yellow spot (usually shaped like triangle) behind eye.

HABITAT:
rivers and lakes with mud bottoms.

False Map Turtle

Graptemys pseudogeographica

SHELL LENGTH:
3½-10¾ in.

WHAT TO LOOK FOR:
carapace brown to olive, often with dark blotches and pale ovals; black-knobbed ridge on carapace; yellow mark behind eye (shape varies from crescent to short bar).

HABITAT:
weedy lakes, rivers, sloughs, reservoirs.

Basking Turtles *Chrysemys, Pseudemys, Trachemys*

Nearly all turtles bask in the sun, but the sunbathing habit is especially marked among members of this group, who often pile on top of one another on a favorite log. The Slider, said to slide speedily into the water when approached, belongs to this group; so do the Painted Turtle, North America's most wide-ranging turtle, and the cooters (*Pseudemys concinna* and *floridana*), two yellow-bellied southeastern species whose name comes from an African word for turtle. One member of the group, the red-eared turtle (a race of the Slider), was once commonly sold in pet shops. Although the needs of pet turtles vary according to species, most require a varied diet ("turtle food" is not adequate), a clean tank, a basking spot, and an understanding of their habits.

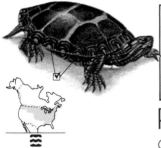

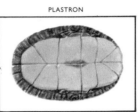

PLASTRON

Painted Turtle
Chrysemys picta

SHELL LENGTH: 4-9¾ in.

WHAT TO LOOK FOR: carapace smooth, olive to black, with red bars or crescents along edge; plastron yellow, sometimes with markings.

HABITAT: shallow, weedy freshwater areas.

Slider
Trachemys scripta

SHELL LENGTH: 5-11½ in.

WHAT TO LOOK FOR:
red, orange, or yellow stripe or patch behind eye; chin rounded on underside; carapace olive to brown, with yellow stripes and bars.

HABITAT: shallow, weedy freshwater areas.

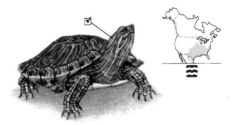

Blanding's Turtles *Emydoidea*

Although the one species in this group is sometimes confused with a box turtle, its long, yellow-throated neck is quite different; and it cannot close its shell as tightly, even though its plastron is hinged. More active in colder weather than most turtles, it has sometimes been seen swimming beneath ice.

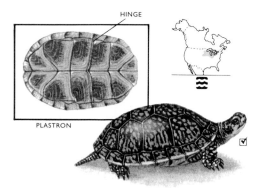

HINGE

PLASTRON

Blanding's Turtle

Emydoidea blandingi

SHELL LENGTH:
5-10½ in.

WHAT TO LOOK FOR:
carapace high, smooth, black, with yellowish spots, blotches, or lines; plastron hinged; chin and throat yellow.

HABITAT:
marshes; shallow, weedy creeks, ponds, lakes.

Turtles, tortoises, and terrapins.

Any reptile with a bony shell and a toothless beak is a turtle. North America has some 50 species, including 3 that belong to the tortoise family. Adapted to life on land, tortoises usually have short legs, webless feet, and high dome-shaped shells. The word "terrapin" has no specific scientific meaning. Instead, it is used as the popular name for several kinds of edible and formerly commercially valuable freshwater turtles.

Gopher Tortoises *Gopherus*

Named for their gopherlike digging habits, the only tortoises in North America have flattened front limbs used in scooping out the dry soil. Two of the North American species, the Desert Tortoise and the Gopher Tortoise, dig a long tunnel with a resting chamber at the end. The third species, Berlandier's Tortoise (*Gopherus berlandieri*), of Texas and Mexico, has a simpler burrow, often just a sloping hole. All three have the slow gait and vegetarian diet typical of tortoises throughout the world.

Desert Tortoise
Gopherus agassizii

SHELL LENGTH:
9-14½ in.

WHAT TO LOOK FOR:
carapace with high dome and deeply incised concentric lines, often with yellow or orange in center; front feet flat, with large scales; hindfeet round, stumpy.

HABITAT:
canyon bottoms, slopes, washes, oases.

Gopher Tortoise
Gopherus polyphemus

SHELL LENGTH:
6-14½ in.

WHAT TO LOOK FOR:
carapace with high dome; front feet flat; hind feet round, stumpy; head large, rounded, grayish black.

HABITAT:
dry, sandy transition zones between grasslands and forests.

Softshell Turtles *Trionyx*

Most turtles have two layers of protective armor—a bony shell and an overlying layer of hard plates. A softshell turtle is not truly soft-shelled, for it too has a bony shell; but instead of the hard plates, soft, leathery skin covers the shell. In the young and in most adult males this skin is dotted with dark circles. The males are much smaller than the females. Softshell turtles spend long periods underwater buried in mud, with their tubular snouts just reaching the water's surface. Two species are widespread: the Spiny Softshell and the Smooth Softshell (*Trionyx muticus*), which inhabits the Mississippi and its tributaries.

Spiny Softshell
Trionyx spiniferus

SHELL LENGTH:
5-18 in.

WHAT TO LOOK FOR:
carapace soft, leathery, thin, flat, with spiny projections along front edge; feet webbed; nose long, tapering.

HABITAT:
fast rivers, lakes, marshy streams, ponds.

Loggerhead Sea Turtles *Caretta*

Sea turtles come ashore (at night and formerly in large numbers) only to lay eggs. The Loggerhead, the species most commonly encountered along the North American coast, follows the typical pattern. After mating in shallow water, the female digs a deep hole in the beach, lays more than a hundred eggs, covers them with sand, and heads out to sea. The eggs hatch about eight weeks later. Sea turtles have been drastically affected by humans. Their large size, large number of eggs, and predictable habits have worked against their survival, as has development in coastal areas.

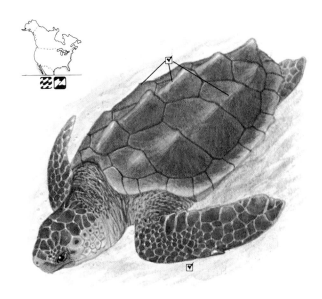

Loggerhead

Caretta caretta

SHELL LENGTH:
31-48 in.

WHAT TO LOOK FOR:
flipperlike limbs; carapace reddish brown, with 3 knobby ridges; 2 pairs of scales between eyes.

HABITAT:
open seas, salt marshes, bays.

Banded Geckos *Coleonyx*

Geckos form a large family of tropical and subtropical lizards. Although many geckos can climb, the banded species are ground dwellers, hiding in rock crevices by day and prowling about at night for insects. Most geckos lack functional eyelids, but the three banded geckos, all residents of the Southwest, have eyelids that open and shut.

Banded Gecko
Coleonyx variegatus

LENGTH:
4½-6 in.

WHAT TO LOOK FOR:
cream, yellow, or pinkish, with brown bands, blotches, or spots; eyes with vertical pupils and prominent, movable lids.

HABITAT:
rocky hillsides, canyons, washes, dunes.

Earless Lizards *Holbrookia*

Unlike snakes and salamanders, most lizards have ear openings through which they hear airborne sounds. Earless lizards do not. Larger than the Lesser Earless Lizard but with a smaller range, the Greater Earless Lizard (*Cophosaurus texanus*) has conspicuous dark bands on the underside of its tail.

Anoles *Anolis*

Abundant in the tropics, anoles are the largest group of reptiles in the Western Hemisphere; there are nearly 200 species. Only the Green Anole is native to North America, although several West Indian species have been introduced into southern Florida. Anoles have enlarged toe pads, enabling the lizards to climb with ease. Like African chameleons, anoles change color in response to changes in light, temperature, and emotional state. Males are highly territorial and drive away rivals with a series of head-bobs, followed by a display of the colorful throat fan.

Green Anole

Anolis carolinensis

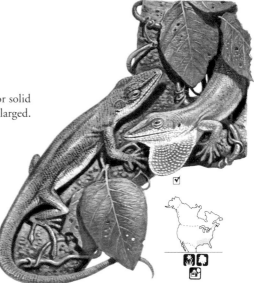

LENGTH:
5-8 in.

WHAT TO LOOK FOR:
usually green (can become mottled or solid brown); pink throat fan; toe pads enlarged.

HABITAT:
trees, shrubs, vines, walls, fences.

◄ Lesser Earless Lizard

Holbrookia maculata

LENGTH: 4-5 in.

WHAT TO LOOK FOR: absence of ear openings; gray to red-brown (similar to soil); 2 rows of dark blotches from neck to tail along each side.

HABITAT: sand and gravel areas in shortgrass prairies; cultivated areas; barren deserts.

Leopard Lizards *Gambelia*

During the day these large, agile lizards wait in the shade of a bush for spiders, insects, and smaller lizards, darting to another bush if nothing passes by. Like collared lizards, a leopard lizard raises its front legs and holds them in front of its body while running at high speed on its hind legs. Elusive and pugnacious, it may hiss if cornered and will bite if picked up. The Blunt-nosed Leopard Lizard (*Gambelia sila*), an endangered species, occurs in California's San Joaquin Valley.

Leopard Lizard

Gambelia wislizenii

LENGTH:
8½-15 in.

WHAT TO LOOK FOR:
body and tail rounded; gray or tan, with brown, leopardlike spots and white bars.

HABITAT:
deserts, dry plains.

Night Lizards *Xantusia*

Despite their name, night lizards are not entirely nocturnal. Although certain species hide under rocks, bark, or decaying plants when the sun is up, the Desert Night Lizard forages for insects during the day and into the evening. Its young are born alive, tailfirst and upside down. Most other lizards hatch from eggs.

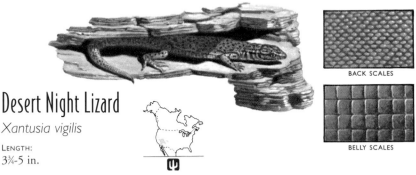

BACK SCALES

BELLY SCALES

Desert Night Lizard
Xantusia vigilis

LENGTH:
3¾-5 in.

WHAT TO LOOK FOR:
eyes with vertical pupils; no eyelids; soft skin; scales on back small, grainy; belly scales large, square; light stripe from eye to neck.

HABITAT: rock outcrops, debris beneath desert plants.

Zebra-tailed Lizards *Callisaurus*

Discretely spotted and rather dull overall, the Zebra-tail blends with its sur-roundings to an extraordinary extent. When frightened, however, it may take on a different appearance, raising and curling its tail and thus exposing the zebralike stripes on the underside as it runs. It is one of North America's fastest lizards and can reach speeds of more than 15 miles an hour over short distances.

Zebra-tailed Lizard
Callisaurus draconoides

LENGTH: 6-9 in.

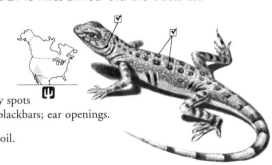

WHAT TO LOOK FOR: 2 rows of dusky spots on back; tail white below, with blackbars; ear openings.

HABITAT: open areas with packed soil.

Collared Lizards *Crotaphytus*

Collared lizards mate in spring and lay eggs in midsummer. The male (shown here), like most lizard males, is more brightly colored than the female. Relatively unusual, though, is that females carrying fertilized eggs develop bright markings on their sides.

Collared Lizard

Crotaphytus collaris

LENGTH:
8-14 in.

WHAT TO LOOK FOR:
large head; black and white bands across neck; color often brilliant; female with orange spots and side stripes in spring.

HABITAT:
rocky hills or mountains with few plants.

Desert Iguanas *Dipsosaurus*

Preferring temperatures above 100°F, the Desert Iguana becomes active toward midday, after most other reptiles in the area have taken refuge from the heat. When the sand becomes unbearably hot, it climbs into a creosote bush to cool itself and eat the vegetation. At night, and also during hibernation, it rests in a rodent burrow whose entrance it has plugged with sand.

Desert Iguana

Dipsosaurus dorsalis

LENGTH:
10-16 in.

WHAT TO LOOK FOR:
low crest of enlarged scales down middle of back; round body; head small, short-snouted.

HABITAT:
creosote-bush desert.

Horned Lizards *Phrynosoma*

Expanded scales on the head, and sometimes also on the sides, give horned lizards (or "toads") a bizarre appearance and protect them from predators as well. If attacked, a horned lizard may open its mouth, hiss, bite, or even eject blood from the corners of its eyes. Horned lizards can remain active at temperatures above 100°F, but when it gets too hot they dig into loose soil by shuffling the body sideways.

Short-horned Lizard

Phrynosoma douglassi

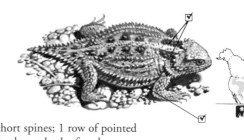

LENGTH:
2½-5¾ in.

WHAT TO LOOK FOR:
flat body; head armed with short spines; 1 row of pointed scales along flanks; 2 dark blotches at back of neck.

HABITAT:
prairies to high mountain forests.

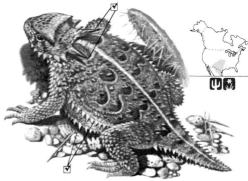

Texas Horned Lizard

Phrynosoma cornutum

LENGTH:
2½-7 in.

WHAT TO LOOK FOR:
flat body; head armed with spines (2 long ones in center); 2 rows of pointed scales along flanks.

HABITAT:
dry, sparsely vegetated flatlands with loose soil.

Spiny Lizards *Sceloporus*

The Eastern Fence Lizard is North America's most widespread lizard. The males, like those of other spiny lizards (18 species occur in the United States and Canada), usually have bright blue belly patches, displayed when they flatten their sides to attract a female or warn off an intruder.

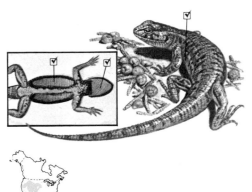

Sagebrush Lizard
Sceloporus graciosus

LENGTH:
5-6 in.

WHAT TO LOOK FOR:
rusty area behind front legs; shoulder usually with black spot; small, grainy scales on back of thigh; males with blue on throat and darker blue on belly.

HABITAT:
sagebrush flats to mountain forests.

Eastern Fence Lizard
Sceloporus undulatus

LENGTH:
3½-7½ in.

WHAT TO LOOK FOR:
body with rough, raised scales; gray to brown, with dark, wavy crossbars or dark and light stripes; males with bluish patches on throat and belly.

HABITAT:
dry woodlands, prairies, brushlands.

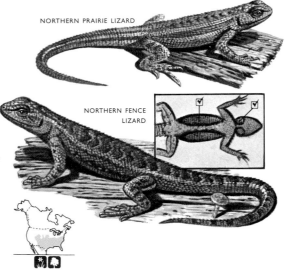

NORTHERN PRAIRIE LIZARD

NORTHERN FENCE LIZARD

Chuckwallas *Sauromalus*

In the morning the Chuckwalla basks until its body temperature reaches about 100° F. Then it forages for flowers, fruits, and leaves. When frightened, this large, timid lizard flees into a rock crevice and inflates its body so that it is wedged in place. Chuckwallas vary widely in appearance. For example, the young have crossbands, which fade with time and disappear entirely on the larger males.

Chuckwalla

Sauromalus obesus

LENGTH:
11-16½ in.

WHAT TO LOOK FOR:
body large, puffy; loose folds of skin at neck and sides; tail thick, blunt-tipped.

HABITAT:
rocky hillsides, outcrops in creosote-bush deserts.

Ground Skinks *Scincella*

One difference between lizards and snakes is that most lizards have eyelids. (A snake's eye is covered by a clear scale and can never close.) Although a lizard's eyelids, like human eyelids, are usually opaque, the lower lids of ground skinks and a few others have a transparent "window," permitting the animal to see while its eyes are closed. This is especially advantageous for creatures that live underground or in other places where loose particles of soil or debris could injure their eyes.

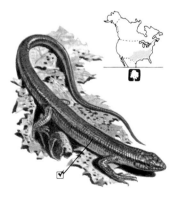

Side-blotched Lizards *Uta*

The Side-blotched Lizard, the only representative of this group in the United States, rises early, warms itself by basking on a rock, and then searches for food. An insatiable eater, it consumes myriads of insects, spiders, and scorpions. It bobs its head to drive off intruders, a habit shared with the spiny lizards. It also looks somewhat like a spiny lizard, but is distinguished by a dark blotch on each side and a loose fold of skin under the throat.

Side-blotched Lizard

Uta stansburiana

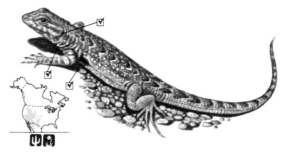

LENGTH:
4-6¼ in.

WHAT TO LOOK FOR:
blue to black blotch behind front leg; fold of skin across throat; ear openings.

HABITAT:
deserts to mountains; sandy or rocky areas with low vegetation or scattered trees.

◄Ground Skink

Scincella lateralis

LENGTH:
3-5 in.

WHAT TO LOOK FOR:
brown lizard with dark side stripe running from eye onto tail; small legs; long tail; smooth, shiny scales.

HABITAT:
humid woods rich in leaf litter.

Skinks *Eumeces*

Like most lizards in temperate parts of North America, these shiny creatures hibernate in soil in winter, court and mate in spring, and lay eggs that hatch in late summer or early fall. The female skink becomes secretive after mating. She hollows out a depression in moist soil or rotting wood, deposits 2 to 21 eggs in the nest, and protects the eggs until they hatch a month or two later. The hatchlings look different from the adults—so different that people once thought they were another species.

Five-lined Skink

Eumeces fasciatus

LENGTH:
5-8 in.

WHAT TO LOOK FOR:
adult with faded stripes and gray tail; breeding male with red-orange jaws; young with 5 light stripes and blue tail.

HABITAT:
damp woods with leaf litter, shaded gardens.

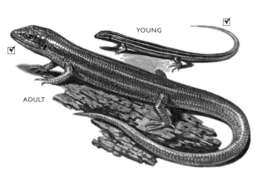

YOUNG

ADULT

Great Plains Skink

Eumeces obsoletus

LENGTH:
6½-13¾ in.

WHAT TO LOOK FOR:
rows of scales angling upward on sides between limbs; adult beige or gray, with dark-edged scales; young shiny black, with small white and orange head spots and blue tail.

HABITAT:
grasslands, mesas, canyons, other rocky areas.

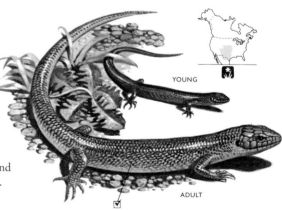

YOUNG

ADULT

Alligator Lizards *Elgaria*

Alligator lizards, like alligators, have a protective armor—in this case, bony plates embedded in the scales. The deep groove along the side of the lizard allows the animal to expand when digesting food or carrying eggs. The glass lizards, which lack legs, have similar plates and grooves.

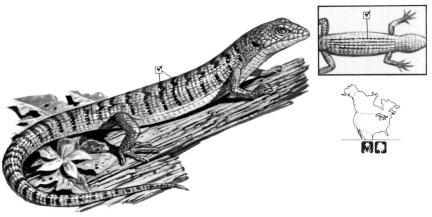

Southern Alligator Lizard

Elgaria multicarinatus

LENGTH:
10-16¾ in.

WHAT TO LOOK FOR:
fold of skin with small scales along lower part of side; back and tail with dark crossbands; dark lines on belly.

HABITAT:
shrubby grasslands to oak and pine woodlands.

Whiptails and Racerunners *Cnemidophorus*

As these long-tailed lizards search for insects and spiders, they move in a rapid, jerky manner and nervously turn their heads from side to side. Like other lizards, both species shown here consist of males and females. But certain other species in the group—the New Mexico Whiptail (*Cnemidophorus inornatus*), for example—are unisexual; all individuals are females, which lay fertile eggs without mating.

Western Whiptail
Cnemidophorus tigris

LENGTH:
8-12 in.

WHAT TO LOOK FOR:
chest with black spots; overall pattern may include light stripes, dark crossbars, or spots; scales on back tiny, grainy; scales on belly large, rectangular.

HABITAT:
deserts to dry woodlands.

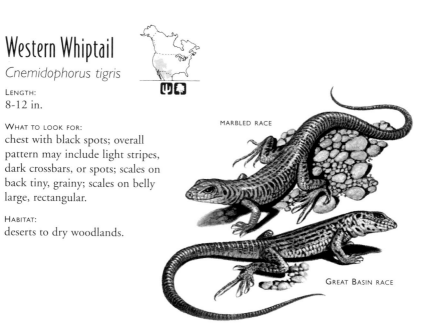

MARBLED RACE

GREAT BASIN RACE

Six-lined Racerunner

Cnemidophorus sexlineatus

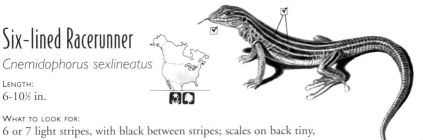

LENGTH:
6-10½ in.

WHAT TO LOOK FOR:
6 or 7 light stripes, with black between stripes; scales on back tiny, grainy; scales on belly large, rectangular; throat blue to green (male) or white (female).

HABITAT:
dry woodlands, grasslands.

Glass Lizards *Ophisaurus*

The tail of a glass lizard is exceptionally fragile, shattering like glass when under stress. An individual with its original tail (the replacement is shorter and darker) is a rare find. People often mistake glass lizards for snakes, but snakes have neither eyelids nor ear openings.

Slender Glass Lizard

Ophisaurus attenuatus

LENGTH:
22-42 in.

WHAT TO LOOK FOR:
legless body; head with eyelids and ear openings; groove along side, with dark speckling or stripes below.

HABITAT:
prairies to woodlands; often near water.

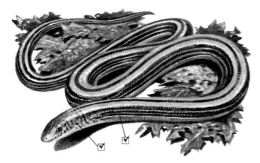

Gila Monsters *Heloderma*

The world's only venomous lizards, the Gila Monster and its close relative the Mexican Beaded Lizard (*Heloderma horridum*), hold on with bulldog tenacity when they bite. The venom, which is produced in glands along the lower jaw, helps subdue potential predators as well as prey. (The lizards feed on rodents and on the eggs and young of ground-nesting birds.) Gila Monsters are active primarily at dusk and after dark, escaping the heat of day in abandoned burrows, under rocks, or in tunnels they have dug themselves.

Gila Monster
Heloderma suspectum

LENGTH:
18-24 in.

WHAT TO LOOK FOR:
heavy body; thick, short, blunt tail; black face and feet; scales beadlike, black, with yellow, orange, or pink.

HABITAT:
rocky, sparsely vegetated areas; canyon bottoms; washes.

Legless Lizards *Anniella*

More abundant than is generally believed, legless lizards may sometimes be found by turning over logs or rocks or raking through surface litter in the appropriate habitat. Much of their life is spent moving in serpentine fashion through loose soil. At dusk and at night they occasionally come to the surface or search the leaf litter below bushes for small insects.

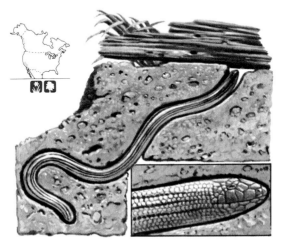

California Legless Lizard

Anniella pulchra

LENGTH:
6-9¼ in.

WHAT TO LOOK FOR:
shovel-shaped snout; no limbs; no ear openings; movable eyelids; shiny scales; back silver or beige, with black lines down middle and along each side; yellow belly.

HABITAT:
moist sand or loam; beaches to pine-oak woodlands.

Worm Lizards *Rhineura*

These burrowing reptiles, found in the United States only in Florida, are not true lizards. Lacking eyes, ear openings, and limbs, they live a largely underground life, sometimes surfacing after heavy rains. People who encounter them while digging or plowing may confuse them with earthworms, but earthworms lack the distinct head and tail.

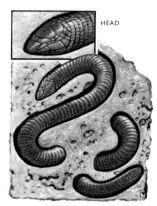

HEAD

Worm Lizard
Rhineura floridana

LENGTH:
7-16 in.

WHAT TO LOOK FOR:
fuchsia-colored, wormlike body; scales in rings around body; tail flat, with small bumps.

HABITAT:
dry, sandy soil; pine or hardwood hammocks.

Blind Snakes *Leptotyphlops*

The tiny eyes of these nocturnal snakes are useless for finding prey. Instead, the reptiles use their sense of smell to locate ants and termites. Normally hidden in moist soil beneath a rock or log, they come to the surface in daylight after a heavy rain. Precise identification requires a close look at the head; the Western Blind Snake (*Leptotyphlops humilis*) has only one scale between its eyes.

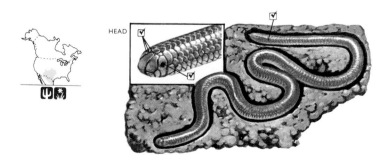

HEAD

Worm Snakes *Carphophis*

Like some three-quarters of the world's 2,700 species of snakes, the Worm Snake belongs to the colubrid family. (*Coluber* is a Latin word for "snake.") Colubrids have well-developed eyes, belly scales as wide as their bodies, and teeth on both jaws. Although a few colubrids are venomous, only two—both African—can inflict fatal bites. Like all colubrids, Worm Snakes are carnivorous; they feed on earthworms.

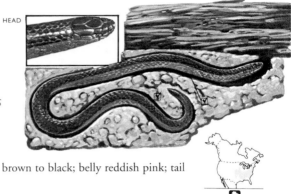

HEAD

Worm Snake

Carphophis amoenus

LENGTH:
8-14¾ in.

WHAT TO LOOK FOR:
round body; back shiny, brown to black; belly reddish pink; tail with sharp spine on tip.

HABITAT:
moist forests; hillsides near streams.

◄Texas Blind Snake

Leptotyphlops dulcis

LENGTH:
5-10¾ in.

WHAT TO LOOK FOR:
body wormlike, shiny; head and tail blunt; eyes tiny, black; scales on belly same size as those on back; large translucent scale over eye; 3 small scales between eyes atop head.

HABITAT:
pockets of moist sand or loam; plains, deserts, rocky hillsides.

Racers *Coluber*

Active by day, the Racer glides swiftly along the ground, holding its head high above the surface. If chased, it often climbs into bushes or trees. When threatened, it vibrates the tip of its tail in dead vegetation, producing a buzzing sound like a rattler. It kills not by constriction, but by pinning down its victim and swallowing it whole.

Racer
Coluber constrictor

LENGTH:
3-6 ft.

WHAT TO LOOK FOR:
slim body; smooth scales; color variable.

HABITAT:
woods, grassy and brushy areas, rocky slopes.

BLUE RACE

WESTERN
YELLOW-BELLIED RACE

Glossy Snakes *Arizona*

Faded Snake is another name for the pallid creature that is the sole member of this group. Like many other desert snakes, it is active mainly at night, leaving its burrow after sundown to search for lizards and small rodents, which it kills by constriction. It lacks the dark belly marks of one of the kingsnakes and the ridged scales of gopher and rat snakes.

Rubber Boas *Charina*

The Rubber Boa is closely related to anacondas and pythons. Like its awesome relatives, it constricts its prey (mammals and birds) until the victim suffocates. Most snakes have no outward sign of limbs, but boas have small remnants ("spurs") on their bellies, used by the male to stroke the female during courtship. Females produce live young, not eggs.

Rubber Boa
Charina bottae

LENGTH:
1-2½ ft.

WHAT TO LOOK FOR:
rubbery body; tip of tail looks like head; large scales on top of head; other scales small, smooth, shiny; eyes small, with vertical pupils.

HABITAT:
damp soil, rotting logs; grasslands to forests.

◀Glossy Snake
Arizona elegans

LENGTH:
2-5½ ft.

WHAT TO LOOK FOR:
scales smooth, shiny; nose slightly pointed; dark line from eye to corner of mouth; belly unmarked.

HABITAT:
deserts, chaparral, woodlands.

Scarlet Snakes *Cemophora*

The eggs of other reptiles are the favorite food of the Scarlet Snake, the single species in this group. Small eggs are eaten whole; bigger ones are torn with its enlarged upper teeth. Scarlet Snakes usually hide beneath rocks or logs during the day.

Scarlet Snake

Cemophora coccinea

LENGTH: 1-2½ ft.

WHAT TO LOOK FOR: snout red, pointed; thin black bands, not encircling body; belly white or yellow, unmarked; compare with coral snakes and "scarlet kingsnake."

HABITAT: forests; nearby fields with loose soil.

Ringneck Snakes *Diadophis*

Although common in many localities, the Ringneck escapes notice because it rarely prowls in the open. Large numbers may congregate in a single hiding place. When disturbed, a Ringneck may coil its tail in a tight spiral, exposing the red belly.

Ringneck Snake

Diadophis punctatus

LENGTH:
1-2½ ft.

WHAT TO LOOK FOR:
back plain olive, gray, brown, or black; neck ring usually present; belly red, orange, or yellowish, often with black spots; scales smooth.

HABITAT:
damp areas in forests, grasslands, deserts; rocky wooded hillsides.

NORTHERN RACE   PRAIRIE RACE

SOUTHERN RACE

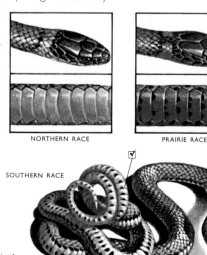

Shovel-nosed Snakes *Chionactis*

With their spadelike snouts, glossy scales, and flat bellies, these snakes can almost swim through the desert soil. Occasionally abroad during the day, they forage mostly at night for insects, spiders, centipedes, and scorpions.

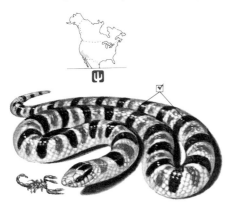

Western Shovel-nosed Snake

Chionactis occipitalis

LENGTH:
10-17 in.

WHAT TO LOOK FOR:
white or yellow, with 21 or more dark bands wholly or partially encircling body (may have partial bands of red between the dark); flat snout.

HABITAT:
mesquite-creosote-bush deserts, sandy washes, dunes, rocky slopes.

Mud and Rainbow Snakes *Farancia*

According to legend, these snakes can hold their tails in their mouths, roll like hoops, and kill people by stinging with their tails. The tail does in fact have a sharp spine, used to subdue struggling prey. The Mud Snake eats amphibians, and the closely related Rainbow Snake (*Farancia erytrogramma*), eels. Brilliantly striped with red and yellow, the Rainbow Snake occupies much the same habitat as the Mud Snake but has a more restricted range.

Mud Snake

Farancia abacura

LENGTH: 3-6¾ ft.

WHAT TO LOOK FOR:
back bluish black; belly with black and pink or red bars extending onto sides; sharp spine on tail.

HABITAT: swampy areas, slow streams, floodplains.

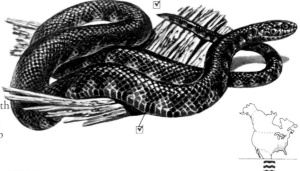

Rat Snakes *Elaphe*

A rat snake, like many other harmless snakes, puts on a show of aggressiveness when cornered. It vibrates its tail, creating a rattling sound in dry vegetation; it hisses and lunges, raising the front part of its body above the ground and drawing its head back in an S-shaped curve. Rat snakes usually crawl on the ground in search of rats and other rodents, thereby earning the friendship of farmers aware of their habits. (They also eat frogs, lizards, birds, and bird eggs.) Rat snakes are superb climbers—an ability enhanced by the special shape of their belly scales. The scales curve upward where they meet the sides, giving the reptiles better traction.

YELLOW RACE

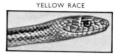

GRAY RACE

BLACK RACE

Rat Snake

Elaphe obsoleta

LENGTH:

3-8 ft.

WHAT TO LOOK FOR:

body fairly stout; belly flat; sides straight (not rounded); belly scales flat in middle, angled where they meet sides; back scales slightly ridged; striped, blotched, or uniformly colored.

HABITAT:

swamps; hardwood forests; rocky, wooded hillsides; farms; suburban woods.

Corn Snake
Elaphe guttata

LENGTH:
2-6 ft.

WHAT TO LOOK FOR:
belly flat; sides straight; belly
scales flat in middle, angled where
they meet sides; arrow-shaped
blotch on head; belly with black
squarish blotches; tail striped on underside.

HABITAT:
pine barrens; rocky, wooded hillsides; groves;
farms; abandoned farm buildings.

"GREAT PLAINS RAT SNAKE"

EASTERN RACE

Indigo Snakes *Drymarchon*

The largest snake in North America has an unusual distribution—a gap of hundreds of
miles separates the two races, which look quite different from one another. Although at
one time the two populations must have been connected, the gap is not of recent ori-
gin and should not be attributed to humans. But human disturbance has caused the cur-
rent decline of the eastern race, shown here with its eggs.

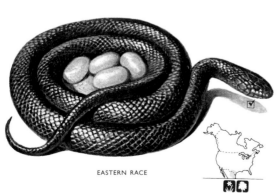

EASTERN RACE

Indigo Snake
Drymarchon corais

LENGTH:
5-8½ ft.

WHAT TO LOOK FOR:
body stout, smooth-scaled,
shiny blue-black; throat, sides
of head orange, red, or cream;
front part of Texas race brownish, with trace of pattern.

HABITAT:
woodlands, orange groves,
thickets, grasslands; near water.

Milk Snakes and Kingsnakes *Lampropeltis*

Although Milk Snakes supposedly milk cows, the snakes in this group actually feed on rodents, birds, lizards, and other snakes, including rattlesnakes and Copperheads. They seize the victim behind the head and surround it with several coils, constricting the prey until it suffocates. The food is consumed headfirst—a typically snakelike way of eating. Loosely joined jaws can stretch, enabling the snake to swallow prey considerably larger than its head. The eastern race of the Milk Snake may be mistaken for a Copperhead, and the scarlet race for a coral snake.

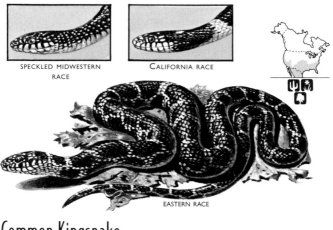

SPECKLED MIDWESTERN RACE

CALIFORNIA RACE

EASTERN RACE

Common Kingsnake

Lampropeltis getula

LENGTH:
3-6½ ft.

WHAT TO LOOK FOR:
scales smooth, glossy, with light-colored centers; chocolate-brown to black, with crossbands, chain links, blotches, stripes, or speckles.

HABITAT:
varied; includes pine woodlands, marshes, swamps, valleys, rocky hillsides, grasslands, deserts, chaparral.

EASTERN RACE

SOUTHEASTERN RACE
("SCARLET KINGSNAKE")

Milk Snake

Lampropeltis triangulum

LENGTH:
1½-4 ft.

WHAT TO LOOK FOR:
Y- or V-shaped light mark behind head, or white or yellow collar around neck and black-bordered red bands separated by white or yellow rings that widen on sides; scales smooth, glossy.

HABITAT:
varied; includes woodlands, rocky hillsides, grasslands, suburbs.

Hognose Snakes *Heterodon*

Various local names—blow viper, puff adder, hissing adder—stem from the belligerent behavior of the Eastern Hognose Snake. If the hissing, lunging, puffed-up body and flattened neck fail to discourage an interloper, the snake rolls over, playing dead. The Western Hognose (*Heterodon nasicus*), a midwestern species with large black belly blotches, puts on a similar but somewhat less impassioned performance.

Eastern Hognose Snake
Heterodon platyrhinos

LENGTH:
1½-3¾ ft.

WHAT TO LOOK FOR:
upturned snout; wide neck; thick body; underside of tail lighter than belly; yellow, brown, tan, or reddish, with dark, squarish blotches on back and round ones on sides; may be all black.

HABITAT:
sandy areas, woodland edges, grasslands.

Coachwhips and Whipsnakes *Masticophis*

Alert and agile, North America's fastest snakes undulate in a series of S-shaped curves—the main way that snakes move. Some snakes can crawl like a caterpillar (this is known as rectilinear motion), move by extending and contracting the body (concertina motion), or slip sideways (sidewinding).

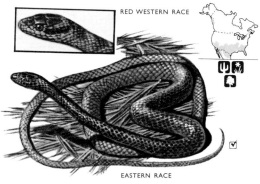

RED WESTERN RACE

EASTERN RACE

Night Snakes *Hypsiglena*

True to its name, the Night Snake searches after dark for lizards and frogs; during the day it hides in crevices or under plant debris. Night Snakes, like most nocturnally active snakes, usually have vertical pupils; day-active snakes generally have round ones. Although not considered dangerous to humans, Night Snakes should be treated with caution; they have enlarged teeth toward the back of the upper jaw.

Night Snake
Hypsiglena torquata

HEAD

LENGTH:
1-2 ft.

WHAT TO LOOK FOR:
large, dark blotch on each side of neck (may meet in center); vertical pupils; dark line behind eye; white scales on upper lip.

HABITAT:
plains, deserts, chaparral, oak-pine woodlands.

◀Coachwhip
Masticophis flagellum

LENGTH:
3-8½ ft.

WHAT TO LOOK FOR:
slim, unstriped body; tail long, sometimes pink on underside or paler than body; smooth scales; overall color varying from black to pink, red, tan, or gray.

HABITAT:
pine woodlands, rocky hillsides, prairies, scrublands, chaparral.

Water and Salt Marsh Snakes *Nerodia*

On sunny days water snakes bask on tree limbs or shrubs overhanging streams and ponds, unnoticed until they slide or drop into the water. Most snakes can swim, but these species are especially adept swimmers and divers, slithering through the water and capturing fish and frogs (both tadpoles and adults). Frequently mistaken for Copperheads or Cottonmouths, they are not venomous but can inflict a painful bite. Snakes use their teeth for holding prey, not for chewing.

Plain-bellied Water Snake

Nerodia erythrogaster

LENGTH: 2½-5 ft.

WHAT TO LOOK FOR: belly red, orange, or yellow; back plain or with dark-bordered light crossbars; stout body; head broad, distinct from neck; scales with ridges.

HABITAT: swamps, forested edges of streams, ponds, lakes.

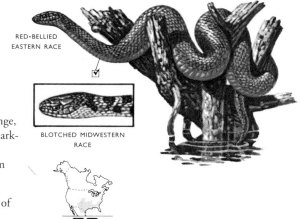

RED-BELLIED EASTERN RACE

BLOTCHED MIDWESTERN RACE

Northern Water Snake

Nerodia sipedon

LENGTH: 2-4 ft.

WHAT TO LOOK FOR: crossbands on neck; dark blotches on back and sides; belly with crescent-like spots, scattered or in 2 rows; stout body; broad head; scales with ridges.

HABITAT: all types of freshwater; tidal marshes.

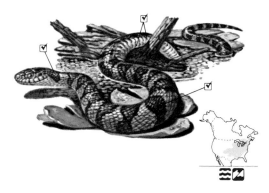

Southern Water Snake

Nerodia fasciata

LENGTH:
1½-5 ft.

WHAT TO LOOK FOR:
back with dark bands; dark line from eye to corner of mouth; belly with squiggles or squarish blotches; stout body; broad head; scales with ridges.

HABITAT:
all types of freshwater; tidal marshes.

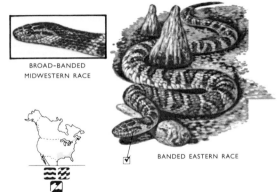

BROAD-BANDED MIDWESTERN RACE

BANDED EASTERN RACE

Green Snakes *Opheodrys*

The eggs of the Smooth Green Snake hatch in 4 to 23 days, a sharp contrast with the several months that most snakes take. In this species the embryos develop to a relatively advanced stage before the eggs are laid. The Rough Green Snake (*Opheodrys aestivus*), a large southern species, has a longer incubation time.

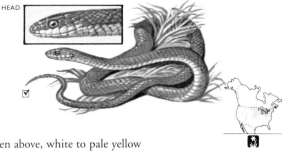

HEAD

Smooth Green Snake

Opheodrys vernalis

LENGTH:
1-2 ft.

WHAT TO LOOK FOR:
slim body; long tail; bright green above, white to pale yellow below; smooth scales.

HABITAT:
damp grass; fields bordering woodlands; streambanks; marshes.

Patch-nosed Snakes *Salvadora*

Unlike most snakes of the arid West, the patch-nosed snakes tolerate high temperatures and are active at midday. Their prey includes lizards, snakes, and small rodents.

Western Patch-nosed Snake
Salvadora hexalepis

LENGTH:
2-3¾ ft.

WHAT TO LOOK FOR:
wide triangular scale curved back over tip of snout; beige or yellow back stripe bordered by dark side stripes.

HABITAT:
deserts, chaparral.

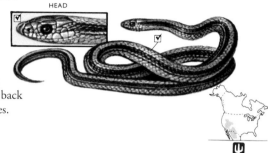

Long-nosed Snakes *Rhinocheilus*

The single species in this group spends most of its life underground or hidden between rocks. At night it emerges to feed on small mammals, small reptiles, and reptile eggs.

Long-nosed Snake
Rhinocheilus lecontei

LENGTH:
2-3 ft.

WHAT TO LOOK FOR:
snout pointed, jutting beyond lower jaw; black blotches flecked with white, alternating with reddish or pink blotches.

HABITAT:
prairies, brushy deserts, chaparral.

Pine Snakes, Bullsnakes, or Gopher Snakes *Pituophis*

All these names refer to the same species, a powerful constrictor that seeks out rodents in their burrows and occasionally climbs trees in search of birds or eggs. Pine Snake is the eastern name; Bullsnake, the midwestern; Gopher Snake, the western. There are several races.

"NORTHERN PINE SNAKE"

"BULLSNAKE"

Pine Snake, Bullsnake, or Gopher Snake
Pituophis melanoleucus

LENGTH:
4-8 ft.

WHAT TO LOOK FOR:
stout body; head relatively small, pointed; scales with ridges; 4 scales across nose in front of eyes (2 in most other snakes); hisses loudly.

HABITAT:
grasslands, brushlands, pine barrens, rocky deserts.

Red-bellied and Brown Snakes *Storeria*

Although common in many parts of their range, these secretive serpents often go unnoticed as they search for worms and slugs beneath rocks, lumber, leaves, and trash. Snakes in this group do not lay eggs. Instead, the female gives birth, in summer and early fall, to some 5 to 18 young, each 3 to 4 inches long.

Red-bellied Snake

Storeria occipitomaculata

LENGTH:
8-16 in.

WHAT TO LOOK FOR:
neck with 3 light spots or collar; belly red, orange, yellow, or black; back brown, with 4 faint dark stripes or 1 wide pale stripe.

HABITAT:
hilly woodlands, damp meadows, bogs.

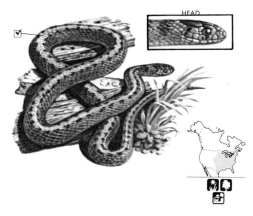

Brown Snake

Storeria dekayi

LENGTH:
10-20 in.

WHAT TO LOOK FOR:
wide, pale back stripe, bordered by rows of dark spots; small black dots along edge of belly; scales with ridges.

HABITAT:
damp woodlands, pond edges, freshwater and saltwater marshes, suburban parks, vacant lots.

Garter and Ribbon Snakes *Thamnophis*

The 13 species of garter snakes ranging over most of the lower 48 states and southern Canada, differ primarily in the pattern of stripes. Snakes in this group produce live young and feed on fish, worms, and other small animals. Like most other reptiles, they molt several times a season. Snakes shed their skins all at once rather than in small pieces. When a snake is about to molt, it loses interest in food. Its eyes cloud over, indicating that new tissue is forming beneath the old. Until its eyes clear, several days before the molt, the snake stays in hiding. Then it begins to move about, rubbing its jaws and snout against rough surfaces. Normally the skin on the head pulls away first. Then the snake winds its way through rock crevices or brush, causing the skin to be pulled away inside-out.

Western Terrestrial Garter Snake

Thamnophis elegans

LENGTH: 1½-3½ ft.

WHAT TO LOOK FOR: 3 stripes, one on back and one on each side; side stripes occupy 2nd and 3rd rows of scales above belly; area between stripes has dark spots or light flecks; overall color variable; 8 upper lip scales (6th and 7th enlarged) on sides.

HABITAT: damp meadows; edges of ponds, lakes, streams.

Eastern Ribbon Snake

Thamnophis sauritus

LENGTH: 1½-3 ft.

WHAT TO LOOK FOR: slim body; 3 bright (usually yellow) stripes against dark background, one on back and one on each side; side stripes occupy 3rd and 4th rows of scales above belly; belly plain, bordered with dark brown.

HABITAT: marshes, damp meadows, weedy edges of ponds, lakes, streams.

Common Garter Snake

Thamnophis sirtalis

LENGTH:
1½-4 ft.

WHAT TO LOOK FOR:
3 stripes, one on back and one on each side; side stripes occupy 2nd and 3rd rows of scales above belly; area between stripes often with double row of black spots or red blotches.

HABITAT:
grasslands, marshes, woodlands, suburban parks; often near water.

RED-SIDED
WESTERN RACE

2 FORMS OF
EASTERN RACE

Earth Snakes *Virginia*

The two earth snakes are small, nondescript burrowers found primarily in the East. As the name implies, the Rough Earth Snake (*Virginia striatula*) has ridged scales instead of the rather even ones of the Smooth Earth Snake. To confirm the identification, scientists count scales. The Smooth Earth Snake has six scales on each side of its upper lip; its cousin, five.

Smooth Earth Snake

Virginia valeriae

LENGTH:
7-13 in.

WHAT TO LOOK FOR:
back gray or brown, with occasional dark flecks; belly white or yellow; scales smooth or with slight ridge.

HABITAT:
moist deciduous forests, suburban woods.

Black-headed and Crowned Snakes *Tantilla*

Though harmless to man, these dark-capped, nocturnal snakes have a saliva that is mildly toxic, helping them subdue such prey as worms and spiders. Of the 13 North American species, only the Plains Black-headed Snake, the Southeastern Crowned Snake (*Tantilla coronata*), and the midwestern Flat-headed Snake (*Tantilla gracilis*) are widespread.

Plains Black-headed Snake

Tantilla nigriceps

HEAD

LENGTH: 7-14¾ in.

WHAT TO LOOK FOR: black cap on head, with rounded or pointed edge; belly white, with pink, red, or orange stripe; back tan to gray.

HABITAT: rocky hillsides, prairies, brushy areas, open woodlands.

Lined Snakes *Tropidoclonion*

A garter snake look-alike, the single species in this group must be viewed belly-up for positive identification—not an easy chore, for Lined Snakes thrash about and discharge a foul-smelling excretion when handled. (Many other snakes also do this.) No snake should be picked up unless you are familiar with the proper method of handling and can also identify the venomous species.

Lined Snake

Tropidoclonion lineatum

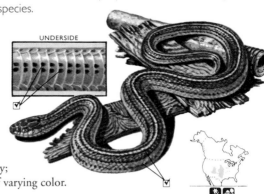

UNDERSIDE

LENGTH: 8-21 in.

WHAT TO LOOK FOR: belly with 2 rows of dark semicircles; central back stripe; side stripes on 2nd and 3rd rows of scales above belly; light to dark gray, with stripes of varying color.

HABITAT: woodland edges, prairie slopes, vacant lots, city parks.

Cottonmouths and Copperheads *Agkistrodon*

Cottonmouths, Copperheads, and rattlesnakes are all pit vipers, snakes with a deep sensory pit between each eye and nostril. Temperature-sensitive receptors in the pits allow the snakes to detect and strike at warm-blooded prey. Pit vipers have long, hollow venom-injecting fangs that fold back against the roof of the mouth when the jaws are closed and move into position as the mouth opens to strike. They give birth to live young, which are venomous from the moment of birth.

Cottonmouth (Water Moccasin)
Agkistrodon piscivorus

LENGTH:
2-6 ft.

WHAT TO LOOK FOR:
stout body; head flat, wider than neck; pit in front of and just below eye; vertical pupils; back plain or with wide, dark, ragged-edged crossbands (young with vivid pattern and yellow tip on tail); mouth white on inside.

HABITAT:
swamps, slow streams, shallow lakes, ditches, rice fields.

Copperhead

Agkistrodon contortrix

LENGTH:
2-4½ ft.

WHAT TO LOOK FOR:
back copper, orange, or pinkish, with bold red-brown crossbands, often narrowing at center of back; plain-colored head; pit in front of and just below eye; vertical pupils.

HABITAT:
rock outcrops and ravines in forests; edges of swamps and floodplains.

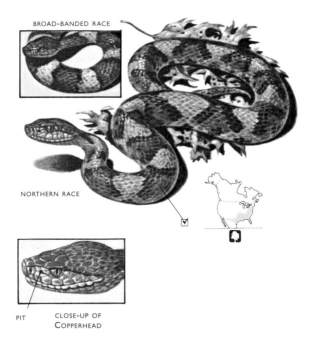

BROAD-BANDED RACE

NORTHERN RACE

PIT   CLOSE-UP OF
           COPPERHEAD

Eastern Coral Snakes *Micrurus*

North America's poisonous snakes fall into two categories. The Arizona Coral Snake (*Micruroides euryxanthus*) and the Eastern Coral Snake have two stationary fangs in the upper jaw; the fangs of snakes in the other group (known as pit vipers) fold back against the roof of the mouth. Coral snake venom affects the nervous and respiratory systems; pit viper venom, blood vessels and red blood cells.

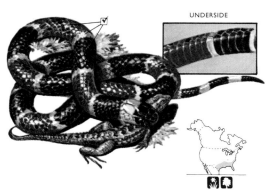

UNDERSIDE

Eastern Coral Snake

Micrurus fulvius

LENGTH:
2-4 ft.

WHAT TO LOOK FOR:
wide red and black bands encircling body, separated by narrow yellow ones (red may be speckled with black); blunt snout; head black to just behind eyes.

HABITAT:
dry woodlands to wet subtropical hammocks; rocky hillsides and canyons in Texas.

Rattlesnakes *Crotalus*

These venomous pit vipers have a warning device at the end of the tail: loosely interlocking segments produce a buzzing noise when the snake is alarmed. Although a new rattle is added each time the snake sheds its skin, the rattles break off frequently and do not indicate age. North America has 13 species, most found west of the Mississippi. One western species, the Sidewinder (*Crotalus cerastes*), has the unusual habit of moving its body sideways in loops, leaving J-shaped tracks in the desert sand.

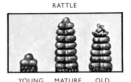

RATTLE

YOUNG   MATURE   OLD

RATTLESNAKE
SHEDDING SKIN

Eastern Diamondback Rattlesnake

Crotalus adamanteus

LENGTH:
3-8 ft.

WHAT TO LOOK FOR:
rattle on tail; back with dark-edged, diamond-shaped blotches surrounded by row of light scales; 2 pale diagonal stripes on side of head; pale vertical lines on snout.

HABITAT:
pine and oak woodlands, abandoned farmlands, saw-palmettos.

Western Diamondback Rattlesnake
Crotalus atrox

LENGTH:
3-7 ft.

WHAT TO LOOK FOR:
tail with rattle and encircling black and white bands; back with pale-bordered diamonds or hexagonal blotches, often faded or sprinkled with dark spots; 2 pale diagonal stripes on cheek.

HABITAT:
dry prairies, brushy deserts, rocky foothills.

Timber Rattlesnake
Crotalus horridus

LENGTH:
3-6 ft.

WHAT TO LOOK FOR:
tail black, with rattle; head wider than neck; northern form all black to predominantly yellow with dark blotches; southern form with tan or red-brown back stripe and dark stripe behind eye.

NORTHERN FORM
(YELLOW PHASE)

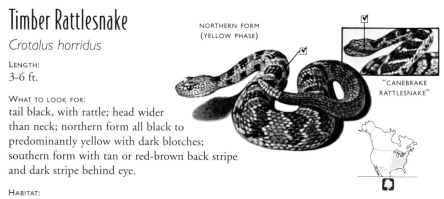

"CANEBRAKE RATTLESNAKE"

HABITAT:
rocky wooded slopes in North; swamps, lowland forests, canebrakes in South.

Western Rattlesnake

Crotalus viridis

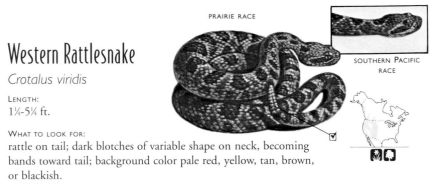

PRAIRIE RACE

SOUTHERN PACIFIC RACE

LENGTH:
1¼-5¼ ft.

WHAT TO LOOK FOR:
rattle on tail; dark blotches of variable shape on neck, becoming bands toward tail; background color pale red, yellow, tan, brown, or blackish.

HABITAT:
prairies to evergreen forests.

Massasaugas and Pygmy Rattlesnakes *Sistrurus*

These small rattlers differ from other rattlesnakes in having nine large scales on top of their heads instead of many small ones. The southeastern Pygmy Rattlesnake (*Sistrurus miliarius*) averages only about 1½ feet long.

Massasauga

Sistrurus catenatus

LENGTH:
1½-3¼ ft.

WHAT TO LOOK FOR:
light-edged dark stripe behind eye; rows of dark blotches in center of back and on sides; thick tail; small rattle.

HABITAT:
wetlands to dry woods in East; wet to dry grasslands in Southwest.

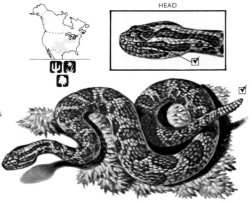

HEAD

Amphibians lead double lives (*amphi* means "both" and *bios* "life"), inhabiting freshwater early in their life cycle and then changing to forms that can live on land. The most pronounced changes—from gills to lungs, from fins to legs, and from a vegetarian diet to an animal one—occur among certain frogs and toads, but many salamanders undergo metamorphosis as well.

Salamanders

North America has more kinds of salamanders than all the other continents combined. The East has the highest concentrations, especially in the Great Smoky Mountains. The West Coast has its own salamander species, but there are few in the Rockies, the desert, or the Central Plains. Glaciers kept them out of the Rockies, and the other places are just too dry.

Salamanders look much like lizards, but their skin is thin and moist (lizards have hard scales or plates), they have only four toes on their front feet (lizards have five), and they have no claws. Being amphibians, salamanders live more in water than lizards, which are reptiles. Though most adults live on land, many species lay their eggs in water.

Eggs laid in water hatch into larvae with tufted external gills. (Eggs laid on land, such as those of the woodland salamanders, bypass this stage.) Several salamanders retain their gills and never leave the water; others, after periods ranging from several months to several years, lose their gills and transform into land-dwelling adults. The adults breathe through their skin or with lungs. Salamanders are carnivorous, feeding on fish, insects, crustaceans, worms, and even small mice.

Finding salamanders takes a bit of searching; they are silent creatures, and most are active only at night. The best times of year to look for them are spring and fall; the best places are under stones in streams and under logs and leaves in moist forests. Some kinds spend much of their time underground, where their surroundings are damper and their enemies fewer than on the surface.

Frogs and Toads
More widespread than salamanders, these lively animals are also less
secretive. But they too are mostly nocturnal, resting during the day in
burrows, in trees, or under leaves, undetected unless they leap out
from under your feet. At night during mating time, however, groups
of singing males loudly announce their presence. A flashlight may help
you to locate some of the songsters, and with a little practice, you may
be able to identify species by their calls. You can even buy recordings
of frog sounds, as you can for birds.

Female frogs and toads tend to be larger than the males. Males
attract them with song, then cling to them and fertilize their eggs as
they shed them in the water. The eggs hatch into "pollywogs"—round-
bellied, long-tailed larvae that, like those of salamanders, have gills on
the outside of the body. In frogs and toads, but not in salamanders,
these external gills are soon covered with skin. So most of the tadpoles
you catch will have no visible gills.

Eventually, in one of nature's most dramatic transformations, the
tadpole metamorphoses into a frog or toad—a tailless terrestrial
creature with long hind limbs and lungs instead of gills. How long
tadpoles stay tadpoles varies with both species and temperature.
Desert-dwelling spadefoot toads may spend a mere two weeks at
this stage, whereas North America's biggest frog, the Bullfrog, may
not metamorphose for several years in the colder parts of its range.

TIPS ON IDENTIFYING AMPHIBIANS

Amphibians include a number of "giveaway" species; recognizing a
Spotted Salamander, a Hellbender, or a Spring Peeper is no difficult
task. For many amphibians, however, you may need to hold the creatures on your hand to check for special markings or structural details.
Among the features important in identifying salamanders are the hind
feet and the grooves in the sides. Frogs and toads often have characteristic protuberances or markings on the head or back, and their feet may
also merit a closer look (toe shape, for example, may be significant).

Mudpuppies and Waterdogs
Necturus

These stubby-tailed salamanders, active mainly at night, hunt small aquatic animals. As is true of most salamanders, males and females look nearly alike. After mating in spring, the female lays dozens of eggs, producing them one by one and placing them under rocks, sticks, or other submerged objects.

Sirens *Siren*

Unlike most amphibians, which transform from aquatic larvae to land-dwelling adults, these creatures remain larvae all their lives. Never leaving the water or losing their bushy external gills, they reproduce in the larval stage. Unlike amphiumas, another group of eellike amphibians of the Southeast, sirens have well-developed front legs and no hind legs.

Mudpuppy

Necturus maculosus

LENGTH:
8-17 in.

WHAT TO LOOK FOR:
body thick, gray to rusty brown, with irregular black spots; tail flattened from side to side; bushy, dark red gills behind head; 4 toes on both front and hind feet.

HABITAT:
canals, streams, rivers, lakes.

Lesser Siren

Siren intermedia

LENGTH:
8-26 in.

WHAT TO LOOK FOR:
eellike body; tail with pointed tip; no hind legs; 4 toes on front feet; stubby or bushy gills just in front of legs.

HABITAT:
weedy ponds; swamps; warm, shallow lakes.

Hellbenders *Cryptobranchus*

The Hellbender is strictly aquatic. Though it has four legs, it does not use them for swimming; instead, it propels itself with its flattened tail. The wrinkles in its skin are believed to supply additional surface for taking in oxygen from the water. Bulkiest of North American salamanders, the Hellbender is dwarfed by its close relative in Japan, the 5½-foot Giant Salamander (*Andrias japonica*). The Hellbender is essentially a river creature, but its Japanese relative inhabits smaller streams.

Hellbender

Cryptobranchus alleganiensis

LENGTH:
12-29 in.

WHAT TO LOOK FOR:
body stocky, gray or brown, with dark spots or mottling; loose flap of skin along each side; broad, flat head.

HABITAT:
clear rivers and streams with rocky bottoms.

Mole Salamanders *Ambystoma*

Mole salamanders burrow into moist ground or leafy debris in a molelike fashion, and they are rarely seen above the surface except on rainy nights or when they congregate around a breeding pond. Their eggs are usually laid in water, though one species, the Marbled Salamander, lays eggs on land. Mole salamanders generally have prominent indentations in their sides, called costal grooves, which mark the spaces between the ribs. The number varies according to species.

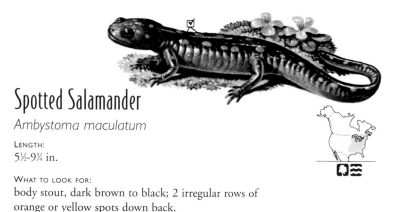

Blue-spotted Salamander
Ambystoma laterale

LENGTH:
3-5 in.

WHAT TO LOOK FOR:
back and sides dark brown to blue-black, with bluish-white patches, spots, or flecks.

HABITAT:
moist deciduous woods.

Spotted Salamander
Ambystoma maculatum

LENGTH:
5½-9¾ in.

WHAT TO LOOK FOR:
body stout, dark brown to black; 2 irregular rows of orange or yellow spots down back.

HABITAT:
woods, hillsides, near water.

Marbled Salamander
Ambystoma opacum

LENGTH:
3½-5 in.

WHAT TO LOOK FOR:
body stocky, grayish to black, with white or silvery crossbars; bars may be joined along sides.

HABITAT:
swampy lowlands to wooded hillsides near temporary ponds.

Long-toed Salamander
Ambystoma macrodactylum

LENGTH:
4-6¾ in.

WHAT TO LOOK FOR:
body slender, dark brown to black; orange, yellow, or green stripe on back; long toes.

HABITAT:
diverse; from sagebrush to moist forests.

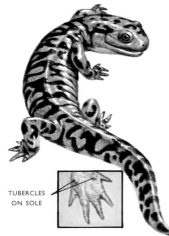

TUBERCLES
ON SOLE

Tiger Salamander
Ambystoma tigrinum

LENGTH:
6-13½ in.

WHAT TO LOOK FOR:
bulky body; broad head; small eyes; highly variable color and pattern (may include light or dark markings); 1 or 2 tubercles on sole of foot.

HABITAT:
diverse; from arid plains to high-elevation forests.

Giant Salamanders *Dicamptodon*

These northwestern salamanders lay clumps of eggs in cool lakes and pools. The newly hatched larvae swim into tributary streams and then take up life on land. Some individuals, however, never transform into land-dwelling adults, reproducing instead while they are aquatic larvae. The Pacific Giant Salamander is the world's largest land salamander. It eats the usual salamander fare of insects and other small animals, but it also preys on snakes and mice.

Pacific Giant Salamander

Dicamptodon ensatus

LENGTH: 7-11¾ in.

WHAT TO LOOK FOR: body heavy, purplish or brown with black mottling; no tubercles on feet.

HABITAT: rivers; adjacent cool, humid forests.

NO TUBERCLES ON SOLE

Dusky Salamanders *Desmognathus*

Dusky salamanders and all salamanders (except newts) described on the following pages lack both gills and lungs as adults. Instead, they breathe through their skins and the lining of their mouths, sometimes pumping their throats rapidly to increase the flow of air. Commonest in the Appalachian Mountains, the dusky salamanders lay grapelike clusters of eggs in soft dirt or shallow excavations near water. Newly hatched larvae may live on land for several weeks before entering the water and completing their development.

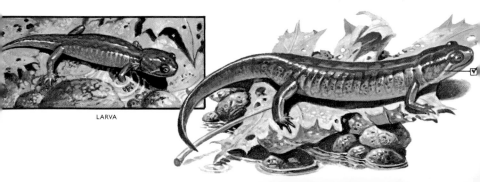

LARVA

Red Salamanders *Pseudotriton*

The Red Salamander and the Mud Salamander (*Pseudotriton montanus*) look much alike and have overlapping ranges. The Mud Salamander, however, has brown eyes and a more snubby snout, and its body is sometimes brownish. In both species the red color is most distinctive in the young and generally fades as the animal matures and develops spots.

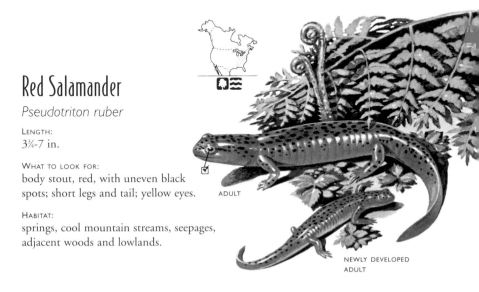

Red Salamander

Pseudotriton ruber

LENGTH:
3¾-7 in.

WHAT TO LOOK FOR:
body stout, red, with uneven black spots; short legs and tail; yellow eyes.

HABITAT:
springs, cool mountain streams, seepages, adjacent woods and lowlands.

ADULT

NEWLY DEVELOPED
ADULT

◄ Dusky Salamander

Desmognathus fuscus

LENGTH: 2½-5½ in.

WHAT TO LOOK FOR: tan to dark brown, with dark mottling or pairs of blotches that may be fused to form a ragged-edged stripe; light line from eye to angle of jaw.

HABITAT: springs, rocky streams, floodplains, adjacent moist areas.

Spring Salamanders *Gyrinophilus*

Like most salamanders, the Spring Salamander (the commonest of this group) is generally good-natured but may try to defend itself by biting. Though it is carnivorous and sometimes even cannibalistic, its teeth are not large enough to inflict an impressive bite.

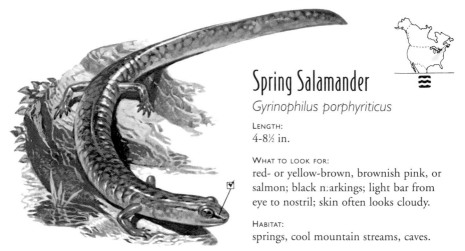

Spring Salamander
Gyrinophilus porphyriticus

LENGTH:
4-8½ in.

WHAT TO LOOK FOR:
red- or yellow-brown, brownish pink, or salmon; black markings; light bar from eye to nostril; skin often looks cloudy.

HABITAT:
springs, cool mountain streams, caves.

Slender Salamanders *Batrachoseps*

Eight species of wormlike salamanders make up this group, most of them limited to particular canyons or forests on the West Coast. When hiding under logs or rocks, a slender salamander generally loops or coils its body. If exposed, it writhes wildly, and its tail often breaks off. Females lay about a dozen eggs on land, which hatch into miniature adults.

California Slender Salamander
Batrachoseps attenuatus

LENGTH: 3-5½ in.

WHAT TO LOOK FOR: body slim, soot-colored, with broad yellow, brownish, or reddish stripe on back; 4 toes on hind feet.

HABITAT: grassy meadows to redwood forests.

Woodland Salamanders *Plethodon*

About two dozen species of woodland salamanders, including some with a range of only a few square miles, inhabit moist woodlands from coast to coast. Though usually slow-moving, they can rise on their legs and run rapidly through the forest. The Red-backed Salamander is a jumper, leaping along by slapping its tail against the ground. Most species exude a white fluid that is distasteful to predators.

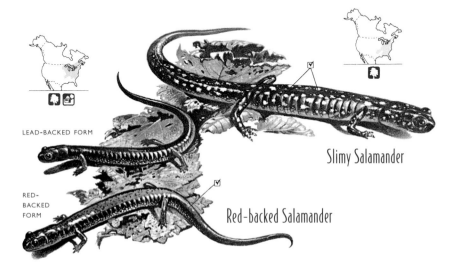

LEAD-BACKED FORM

RED-
BACKED
FORM

Slimy Salamander

Red-backed Salamander

Red-backed Salamander

Plethodon cinereus

LENGTH: 2½-5 in.

WHAT TO LOOK FOR: slender body; red-backed form with wide, straight-edged reddish stripe on back that extends from head well onto tail; lead-backed form with light to dark gray back.

HABITAT: deciduous to coniferous forests.

Slimy Salamander

Plethodon glutinosus

LENGTH: 4½-8 in.

WHAT TO LOOK FOR: shiny black body, with white or yellowish spots on sides; small silvery spots scattered on head, back, tail.

HABITAT: moist ravines, wooded flood-plains, shale banks.

Ensatina Salamanders *Ensatina*

When first exposed from its hiding place, the Ensatina Salamander stands high on its legs, arches its back, and secretes a sticky white fluid from glands in its back and tail. The tail pops off if it is grabbed. Tail length differs between the sexes; the male's is longer, measuring at least the length of the body. The single species in this group shows an astounding range of color and pattern.

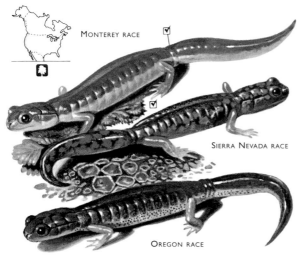

MONTEREY RACE ☑

SIERRA NEVADA RACE

OREGON RACE

Ensatina Salamander
Ensatina eschscholtzi

LENGTH:
3-5¾ in.

WHAT TO LOOK FOR:
tail constricted at base; 5 toes on hind feet; leg color lighter at base than at end.

HABITAT:
cool damp forests; shaded canyons.

Eastern Newts *Notophthalmus*

EFT

Newts lack the side grooves typical of most salamanders. Both the Eastern Newt and the southeastern Striped Newt (*Notophthalmus perstriatus*) lay eggs in water in spring. The larvae remain aquatic until late summer, then lose their gills and transform into red, land-dwelling creatures known as efts. After one to three years, the efts become drab-looking adults and return to the water to mate. The adults never go back to land. A third species, the Black-spotted Newt (*Notophthalmus meridionalis*) of Texas, has no eft stage.

ADULT

Pacific Newts *Taricha*

When attacked by a bird, snake, or other predator, a Pacific newt lifts its head and tail and displays the bright warning colors on its underside. If the predator ignores this warning and puts the newt into its mouth, it receives a further check; the "warts" on the salamander's skin are clumps of glands that give off an irritating secretion. Pacific newts, unlike eastern ones, do not go through a land-dwelling eft stage.

Rough-skinned Newt

Taricha granulosa

LENGTH:
5-8½ in.

WHAT TO LOOK FOR:
rough, warty skin; dark brown back; yellow or red-orange belly; dark lower eyelids.

HABITAT:
slow-moving streams, ponds, lakes; adjacent grasslands and forests.

◄ Eastern Newt (Red Eft)

Notophthalmus viridescens

LENGTH: 2½-5½ in.

WHAT TO LOOK FOR: aquatic adult olive-green to dark brown, with many black dots on yellow belly; land-dwelling eft varies from bright orange to reddish brown; both may have red markings on back.

HABITAT: quiet, weedy ponds, lakes, backwaters; moist woodlands.

Brook Salamanders *Eurycea*

Brook salamanders typically go through an elaborate spring courtship. For up to an hour or more, the male rubs the female with his chin, and the two intertwine their tails. Then the male moves off a short distance and deposits a packet of sperm, which is promptly picked up by the female and stored in her body until the eggs are laid. (This is the usual type of reproduction among salamanders.) In autumn she deposits her eggs under a submerged log or rock. Some brook salamanders are cave dwellers, with pale skin and tiny eyes.

Long-tailed Salamander
Eurycea longicauda

LENGTH: 4-7¾ in.

WHAT TO LOOK FOR:
tail whiplike, longer
than body; northern race yel-
low to orange, with vertical black bars
on tail; southern race has narrow black stripe
inside broad yellow back stripe; western race has
wide, black-speckled yellowish back stripe and
yellow-spotted grayish- to reddish-brown sides.

HABITAT: cave entrances, springs, brooks, floodplains.

NORTHERN RACE

SOUTHERN RACE

Two-lined Salamander
Eurycea bislineata

LENGTH: 2½-4¾ in.

WHAT TO LOOK FOR: back with broad yellow, greenish, or bronze stripe, bordered by dark stripe from eye to tail; tail flattened from side to side.

HABITAT: brooks, seepages, swamps, floodplains; damp high-elevation forests.

Climbing Salamanders *Aneides*

With flattened suctionlike tips on their toes, these salamanders can cling to vertical surfaces and climb trees or rock walls. They are land animals whose eggs hatch directly into diminutive adults, without going through an aquatic larval stage. Of the five species, only the Green Salamander occurs east of the Mississippi.

Green Salamander
Aneides aeneus

LENGTH: 3-5½ in.

WHAT TO LOOK FOR: green blotches on black skin; head looks swollen behind eyes; tips of toes expanded, squarish.

HABITAT: damp crevices in sandstone cliffs and under bark.

Four-toed Salamanders *Hemidactylium*

The tail of the Four-toed Salamander breaks off easily at a conspicuous grooved or pinched-in area at its base. The severed portion continues to wriggle, generally satisfying the attacker (perhaps a Raccoon or fox) while the salamander makes its escape. A new tail soon grows to but the replacement has no bones. This species is one of the few salamanders with four rather than five toes on the hind feet.
All salamanders have four toes on their front feet.

Four-toed Salamander
Hemidactylium scutatum

LENGTH: 2-4 in.

WHAT TO LOOK FOR: red-brown back; gray sides; belly white, with black spots; pinched-in area at base of tail; hind feet with 4 toes.

HABITAT: sphagnum bogs, adjacent moist hardwood forests.

Narrow-mouthed Toads *Gastrophryne*

Narrow-mouthed toads spend most of the day in burrows or under rocks, logs, or debris, emerging at night to feed on ants. These secretive creatures have a distinctive shape: their bodies are bulbous, their snouts pointed, and their heads narrow, with a fold of skin across the back. The tadpoles of this species are also relatively easy to recognize—the mouth is surrounded by a soft disk instead of the hard jaws typical of most tadpoles. In general, frog and toad tadpoles are difficult to sort out. Identification usually requires looking not only at the tadpole's mouth but also at its spiracle (the exit hole for water used in breathing) and vent (anal opening).

Eastern Narrow-mouthed Toad
Gastrophryne carolinensis

LENGTH: 1-1½ in.

WHAT TO LOOK FOR:
tiny head with pointed snout; fold of skin on back of head; color variable; belly spotted with gray.

HABITAT:
moist areas, including leaf litter, rotting logs, burrows, and under rocks.

Frog or toad? With their long legs and tailless bodies, adult frogs and toads are easy to tell apart from other amphibians. But the distinction between animals commonly called frogs and those called toads is less precise.

- Frogs are generally slim and speedy; toads, fat-bodied and rather sluggish.
- Frog skin is usually smooth. Toads have warts.
- Most frogs usually live in or near water. Adult toads may occur in drier habitats.
- Both frogs and toads usually lay eggs in water. Frog eggs are laid in clumps; toads' in strings (usually double strands).

Great Plains Narrow-mouthed Toad

Gastrophryne olivacea

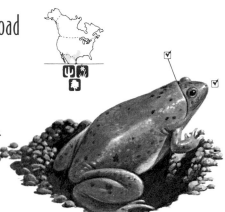

LENGTH:
1-1½ in.

WHAT TO LOOK FOR:
tiny head with pointed snout; fold of skin
across back of head; white, unmarked belly.

HABITAT:
deserts, grasslands, woodlands; in moist
burrows or under rocks or logs.

Tailed Frogs *Ascaphus*

The usual pattern among frogs and toads is that the two sexes find one another by
sound; the males, often equipped with inflatable vocal sacs, attract the females by
singing in chorus. Tailed Frogs, also known as Tailed Toads, inhabit mountain streams,
where the noise of the rushing water obscures other sounds. These amphibians are
not known to utter any sound, but are believed to crawl along the stream bottom
until they find a mate.

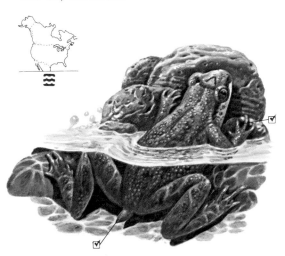

Tailed Frog

Ascaphus truei

LENGTH:
1-2 in.

WHAT TO LOOK FOR:
small bumps on skin; long,
slender front toes; vertical
pupils; short "tail" on male; no
external eardrum.

HABITAT:
swift, cold, clear mountain
streams.

Spadefoot Toads *Scaphiopus, Spea*

These fat, relatively smooth-skinned toads use the hard spades on their hind feet to dig burrows in sand or loose dirt. As they dig, they progress backwards into the excavations and shuffle rapidly out of sight. Spadefoots come out at night to hunt insects and other small animals, and to congregate at aquatic breeding sites. The males utter loud, harsh, nasal calls audible over long distances; females grunt more quietly in response. After mating, the female toads lay masses of eggs on submerged vegetation. The entire development—from egg to tadpole to adult—may take as little as two weeks, the shortest time for any North American toad or frog. Spadefoots usually live in dry environments, breeding in pools of rainwater that disappear quickly. Their accelerated development means that the toads spend a minimum of time in the stages that require water for survival.

SICKLE-SHAPED SPADE
ON HIND FOOT

WEDGE-SHAPED SPADE
ON HIND FOOT

Eastern Spadefoot

Scaphiopus holbrooki

LENGTH:
1¾-3¼ in.

WHAT TO LOOK FOR:
stout body; sickle-shaped "spade" on inner side of hind foot; front toes slightly webbed; eyes with vertical pupils; irregular pale lines often extend backward from eyes.

HABITAT:
sandy, gravelly, or loamy soils; from farmland to forest.

HIND FOOT

Plains Spadefoot

Spea bombifrons

LENGTH:
1½-2½ in.

WHAT TO LOOK FOR:
plump body; black, wedge-shaped "spade" on inner side of hind foot; front toes slightly webbed; eyes with vertical pupils; bony hump between eyes.

HABITAT:
sandy or gravelly shortgrass prairies.

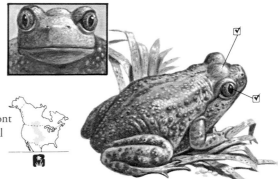

Western Spadefoot

Spea hammondi

LENGTH:
1½-2½ in.

WHAT TO LOOK FOR:
plump body; black, wedge-shaped "spade" on inner side of hind foot; front toes slightly webbed, eyes with vertical pupils; no bony hump between eyes.

HABITAT:
dry plains, mountain valleys, floodplains.

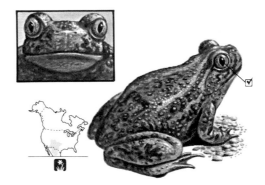

True Toads *Bufo*

Included in this group are about 20 species, ranging in size from the 1-inch Oak Toad to the 9-inch Giant, or Marine, Toad (*Bufo marinus*), a tropical species now well established in Texas and Florida. Most true toads have prominent bony ridges (called cranial crests) on top of their heads, and conspicuous swellings (parotoid glands) behind their eyes. The parotoid glands are a defense against predators, for they secrete fluids that are toxic if taken internally. The warts exude a similar toxin. Despite the prevalent myth, toads do not cause warts in humans and are not poisonous to the touch.

At breeding time (usually spring and summer), large numbers of toads congregate at quiet bodies of water. The males, often distinguished by dark throats and dark pads on some of their toes, call loudly. (The singing of each species is characteristic.) To mate, a male climbs astride a female's back and clasps her firmly, his hold facilitated by the rough pads on his toes. The pair floats together for some time. The female lays strings of eggs, which are fertilized as they pass from her body. After mating, the adult toads may move far from water. Unlike frogs, toads have a thick skin, which reduces water loss and permits survival in dry areas.

True toads, like many other amphibians, eat plants as larvae (tadpoles) and insects as adults. The adult's long tongue, attached at the front of the mouth, can be flipped out to its full length to catch a crawling or flying insect. At times toads also eat fruits and vegetables, and individuals living around houses will feast on dogfood set out for pets. As insect eaters, toads in gardens or elsewhere should be valued for pest control.

Great Plains Toad

Bufo cognatus

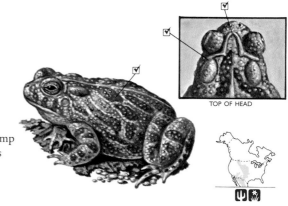

TOP OF HEAD

LENGTH:
2-4½ in.

WHAT TO LOOK FOR:
large dark blotches (often paired), with light borders; cranial crests meet at bony hump on snout; oval parotoid glands touch crests behind eyes.

HABITAT:
grasslands to brushy deserts.

CRANIAL CREST

PAROTOID GLAND

American Toad

Bufo americanus

LENGTH: 2-4¼ in.

WHAT TO LOOK FOR: 1 or 2 brown to orangish warts in each dark spot on back; parotoid gland behind eye elongated, usually separated from cranial crest (sometimes connected by short spur); overall color highly variable.

HABITAT: diverse; from suburban gardens to mountain forests.

Western Toad

Bufo boreas

LENGTH: 2½-5 in.

WHAT TO LOOK FOR: reddish warts surrounded by dark blotches; thin, light line down middle of back; oval parotoid gland behind eye; no cranial crest.

HABITAT: diverse; from arid lowlands to woodland mountain meadows.

Red-spotted Toad

Bufo punctatus

LENGTH:
1½-3 in.

WHAT TO LOOK FOR:
warts with yellowish-orange to red tips; head small and flat; round parotoid glands; cranial crests absent or poorly defined.

HABITAT:
grasslands to desert canyons; near water.

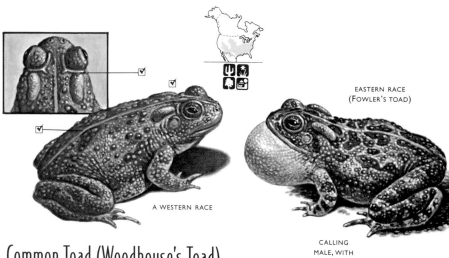

EASTERN RACE
(FOWLER'S TOAD)

A WESTERN RACE

CALLING
MALE, WITH
INFLATED
VOCAL SAC

Common Toad (Woodhouse's Toad)

Bufo woodhousei

LENGTH:
2½-5 in.

WHAT TO LOOK FOR:
light line down middle of back; cranial crests prominent, touching elongated parotoid glands; eastern race has 3 or more warts in each dark spot on back; western races have variable spots and warts.

HABITAT:
sandy areas near freshwater.

Oak Toad

Bufo quercicus

LENGTH:
¾-1¼ in.

WHAT TO LOOK FOR:
small size; distinct white to orange line down middle of back; 4 or 5 pairs of dark blotches on back; parotoid glands elongated; cranial crests poorly developed.

HABITAT:
scrubby oak forests and pinelands.

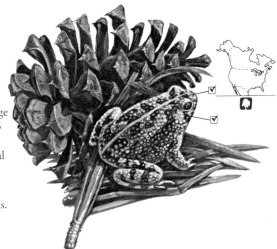

Southern Toad

Bufo terrestris

LENGTH:
1½-4¼ in.

WHAT TO LOOK FOR:
usually brown (color ranges from gray to brick-red); warts often with spines; cranial crests high, with prominent knobs.

HABITAT:
sandhills or oak woods.

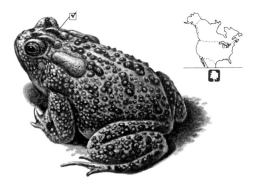

Cricket Frogs *Acris*

Like so many sounds of the wilderness, the mating call of a male cricket frog says different things to different people. To some it echoes the melodious chirp of a cricket; to others, the clacking together of stones or pieces of metal. The calls are commonly heard around ponds and lakes from spring through midsummer and sometimes even later in the southern part of the range. After mating, the female lays 200 or more eggs, singly rather than in clumps like most frogs. By autumn the tadpoles have transformed into froglets. Cricket frogs live in plant cover along the water's edge and are active at night as well as during the day. They jump into the water quickly if disturbed, turn while swimming underwater, and come back to shore at some other point.

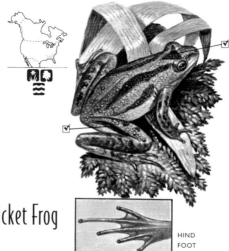

Southern Cricket Frog
Acris gryllus

HIND FOOT

LENGTH:
½-1¼ in.

WHAT TO LOOK FOR:
rough skin (color variable); dark triangle between eyes; dark, sharp-edged stripe on back of thigh; web on hind foot does not reach tip of first toe or next-to-last joint of longest toe.

HABITAT:
in vegetation at edges of marshes, swamps, ponds, ditches, and streams.

Northern Cricket Frog

Acris crepitans

LENGTH:
½-1½ in.

WHAT TO LOOK FOR:
warty skin (color variable); dark triangle between eyes; dark, ragged-edged stripe on back of thigh, fuzzier in midwestern race; web on hind foot reaches tip of first toe and next-to-last joint of longest toe.

HABITAT:
mudflats; edges of shallow ponds, streams, floodplains.

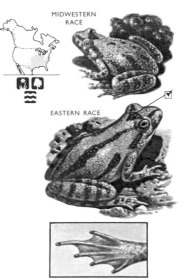

MIDWESTERN RACE

EASTERN RACE

HIND FOOT

Chorus Frogs *Pseudacris*

These small, slim-legged frogs are most conspicuous in the breeding season, when the males gather around ponds and produce a near-deafening clamor. The 11 species belong to the treefrog family, but they have nearly webless toes, and some have very small toe disks.

Striped Chorus Frog

Pseudacris triseriata

LENGTH:
¾-1½ in.

WHAT TO LOOK FOR:
smooth skin; 3 dark stripes (may be broken) on back; dark eye stripe; light stripe on upper lip; tips of toes small, round.

HABITAT:
grasslands to woodland swamps.

HIND FOOT

Treefrogs *Hyla*

Equipped with large suction pads at the tips of their toes, treefrogs have the unfroglike ability to climb vertical surfaces. Most of the 10 species are small (2 inches long or less) and even a leaf is strong enough to support the weight of one. Perched on vegetation near water, the males sing loudly at night or on cloudy, rainy days in spring. Their calls are clear and melodious. The females lay eggs that float at the surface in thin films, with several to several dozen eggs in each patch. Within a week, the eggs hatch into tiny tadpoles; within two months, the tadpoles transform into adults. Most adult treefrogs can change their color or pattern in response to variations in temperature, light, or humidity, although the process may take as long as an hour. The color changes occur in captive animals as well as wild ones, adding to the attractiveness of these diminutive creatures as terrarium pets. Prospective owners should be aware, however, that treefrogs require live insect food and a good deal of care to survive for any length of time in an artificial environment.

HIND FOOT

GREEN COLORATION

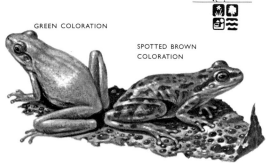

SPOTTED BROWN
COLORATION

Squirrel Treefrog

Hyla squirella

LENGTH: 1-1½ in.

WHAT TO LOOK FOR: skin smooth, varying from green to brown; may have poorly defined, light stripe on sides of body.

HABITAT: trees, shrubs; from suburbs to pine flatwoods.

Barking Treefrog

Hyla gratiosa

LENGTH: 2-2¾ in.

WHAT TO LOOK FOR: skin rough, varying in color from green to brown and usually with round dark spots; light stripe from upper jaw extends along sides of body.

HABITAT: in trees or shrubs near pools or ponds, in burrows, or floating on water.

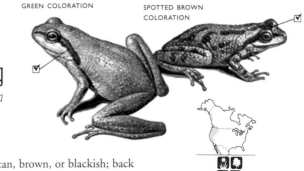

GREEN COLORATION

SPOTTED BROWN
COLORATION

Pacific Treefrog
Pseudacris regilla

LENGTH:
¾-2 in.

WHAT TO LOOK FOR:
skin rough, green, tan, brown, or blackish; back
sometimes with dark markings; black eye stripe;
dark triangle often present between eyes.

HABITAT:
usually in rocks or low plants near water; rarely
high above ground.

CALLING MALE, WITH
INFLATED VOCAL SAC

Spring Peeper
Pseudacris crucifer

LENGTH:
¾-1¼ in.

WHAT TO LOOK FOR:
smooth skin; dark X on back; dark bar
between eyes.

HABITAT:
usually in low plants near temporary
pools in thickets and woodlands.

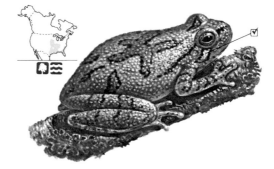

Gray Treefrog
Hyla versicolor

LENGTH:
1¼-2¼ in.

WHAT TO LOOK FOR:
warty skin; light, dark-edged mark below eye; inner surface of hind thigh bright orange or yellow, mottled with black.

HABITAT:
trees and shrubs near woodlands, usually near permanent body of water.

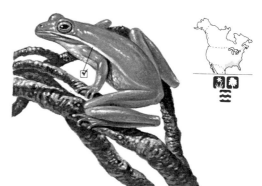

Green Treefrog
Hyla cinerea

LENGTH:
1¼-2½ in.

WHAT TO LOOK FOR:
skin smooth, yellow to green; white or yellow stripe usually present on upper jaw and sides of body; back often with tiny gold spots edged with black.

HABITAT:
in trees and shrubs near lakes, ponds, swamps, streams.

True Frogs *Rana*

These are the typical pond frogs, once almost unbelievably abundant but now much less common because of widespread pollution and the destruction of wetland habitats. The 26 species are rather similar in appearance, with a greenish or brownish color and irregularly shaded dark spots or splotches on their bodies. One important identifying characteristic is the presence or absence of dorsolateral ridges, a pair of folds that run down the back of certain species. The Green Frog has dorsolateral ridges; the Bullfrog, the largest frog in North America, looks quite similar but lacks these folds. Originally found only in the eastern part of the continent, the Bullfrog has been released in suitable locations throughout North America and has also escaped from "farms" where it has been raised for food or other purposes. The deep, sonorous *jug-o-rum* mating calls of the males are familiar spring sounds, so loud and booming that they drown out the weaker calls of smaller species. Male Bullfrogs sing solos rather than joining in choruses like most frogs.

FROG WITH DORSOLATERAL RIDGES

Bullfrog

Rana catesbeiana

LENGTH:
3½-8 in.

WHAT TO LOOK FOR:
large size; smooth skin; ridge extends from eye around large eardrum but not along back; webbing on hind foot does not extend to tip of longest toe.

HABITAT:
any permanent body of freshwater.

TADPOLE

Pickerel Frog

Rana palustris

LENGTH:
1¾-3¼ in.

WHAT TO LOOK FOR:
parallel rows of square blotches; light stripe on jaws; yellow ridges; inner surface of thigh bright yellow to orange.

HABITAT:
cool, clear woodland streams, ponds, lakes; adjacent wet meadows; southern swamps.

UNDERSIDE OF HIND LEG

Wood Frog

Rana sylvatica

LENGTH:
1¼-3¼ in.

WHAT TO LOOK FOR:
pink, tan, reddish brown, or dark brown; dark mask; light line on upper jaw; prominent ridges.

HABITAT:
damp shady woodlands; open areas in far north.

Red-legged Frog

Rana aurora

LENGTH:
2-5¼ in.

WHAT TO LOOK FOR:
red-brown to gray, with black flecks and blotches; distinct ridges; dark mask; light jaw stripe; underside of leg reddish yellow.

HABITAT:
ponds, lakes, streams, adjacent woods.

UNDERSIDE OF HIND LEG

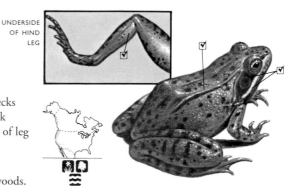

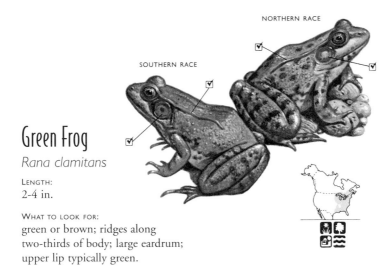

NORTHERN RACE

SOUTHERN RACE

Green Frog
Rana clamitans

LENGTH:
2-4 in.

WHAT TO LOOK FOR:
green or brown; ridges along
two-thirds of body; large eardrum;
upper lip typically green.

HABITAT:
wetlands, streams.

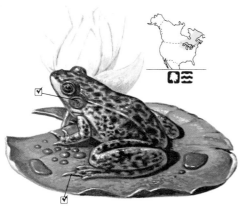

Mink Frog
Rana septentrionalis

LENGTH:
1½-3 in.

WHAT TO LOOK FOR:
large eardrum; hind legs spotted or
blotched; web reaches last joint of
longest hind toe; musky odor; ridges
may be absent.

HABITAT:
cold lakes, ponds.

Northern Leopard Frog

Rana pipiens

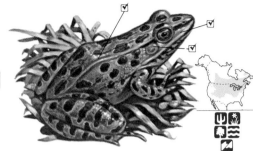

LENGTH:
2-5 in.

WHAT TO LOOK FOR:
green or brown; large, round, light-bordered spots on
back; light-colored ridges; light stripe on upper jaw;
no light spot in center of eardrum.

HABITAT:
damp meadows; weedy edges of streams and lakes;
brackish marshes.

Southern Leopard Frog

Rana sphenocephala

LENGTH:
2-5 in.

WHAT TO LOOK FOR:
green or brown, with dark spots that lack light border;
slender head; pointed snout; light-colored ridges; light
stripe on upper jaw.

HABITAT:
shallow freshwater; nearby areas with dense vegetation;
slightly brackish marshes.

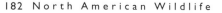

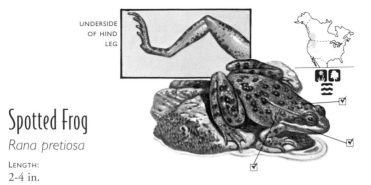

UNDERSIDE OF HIND LEG

Spotted Frog

Rana pretiosa

LENGTH:
2-4 in.

WHAT TO LOOK FOR:
eyes slightly upturned; dark spots with light centers; light jaw stripe; underside of hind leg yellowish to orange-red; ridges present.

HABITAT:
permanent bodies of cold freshwater.

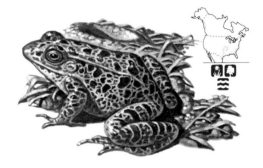

Crawfish Frog

Rana areolata

LENGTH:
2¼-4½ in.

WHAT TO LOOK FOR:
fat-bodied; short, wide head and short legs; skin smooth or warty; many dark markings on back and sides.

HABITAT:
floodplains, wet meadows, sandhills; burrows of crayfish, gopher tortoises, and small mammals.

Index

Credits and acknowledgments for the original edition of
NORTH AMERICAN WILDLIFE

Staff
Editor: Susan J. Wernert
Art Editor: Richard J. Berenson
Associate Editors: James Dwyer, Sally French
Designers: Ken Chaya, Larissa Lawrynenko
Contributing Editor: Katharine R. O'Hare
Contributing Copy Editor: Patricia M. Godfrey

Consulting Editor
Durward L. Allen
Professor of Wildlife Ecology
Department of Forestry and Natural Resources
Purdue University

Consultants
John L. Behler
Curator of Herpetology
New York Zoological Society

James Doherty
General Curator
New York Zoological Society

Alton A. Lindsey
Emeritus Professor of Ecology
Purdue University

Mark MacNamara
Associate Curator of Mammalogy
New York Zoological Society

Robert O. Petty
Associate Professor of Biology
Wabash College

E. M. Reilly, Jr.
Senior Scientist in Zoology
New York State Museum

Contributing Artists
Biruta Akerbergs
Eva Cellini
John D. Dawson
John Hamberger
Lorelle Raboni
Karen Lidbeck Stewart